Val

ONE DAY I'

One Day I'll See You

JENNIFER DOE

KINGSWAY PUBLICATIONS

EASTBOURNE

Front cover design by John Billingham

British Library Cataloguing in Publication Data

Doe, Jennifer
  One day I'll see you
  1. Abortion
  I. Title
  363.46

ISBN 0–86065–769–8

Printed in Great Britain for
KINGSWAY PUBLICATIONS LTD
1 St Anne's Road, Eastbourne, E Sussex BN21 3UN
by Richard Clay Ltd, Bungay, Suffolk.
Typeset by Watermark, Hamilton Road, Cromer

This book is
dedicated to my son Tom

With all my love

Foreword

I have written this book under a pen name in order to
protect those whom I love and whose own stories are
part of this one. In America, people who are nameless,
or who must remain anonymous, are publicly called
'John Doe' or 'Jane Doe'. Infants are referred to as
'Baby John' or 'Baby Jane Doe'. Our aborted children
are, in a sense, all John and Jane Does. They are
anonymous, mostly nameless and largely forgotten. I
have used the name Jennifer Doe as a way of associat-
ing myself with them. It seems appropriate too that
this name could apply to any one of the thousands of
anonymous women, the mothers of these children,
whose pain and loss is also ignored and forgotten.

Public awareness of what abortion really entails is
very limited. There is even less awareness of the aftermath, post-abortion trauma, which thousands of
women must live through. And there is least understanding of all about the possibility of real and complete healing after abortion. I hope that this book will
add something to our understanding of all these areas.

I wrote it for many people; for those who do not
know, or do not want to know, what abortion can do to
a woman; for those who do realise what abortion really

is but do not believe that a woman can ever recover from it; for those who believe that a woman should not recover from it, who believe that she ought to continue suffering; for those who are trying to offer help and comfort to women suffering from post-abortion distress. For all these, and for different reasons, there is a real need to understand what abortion does to the ones who are left behind and why. Most of all, however, I wrote it for those who are suffering now, because their children have been killed by abortion.

I set out neither to minimise the reality of killing an unborn child nor to stand in judgement upon those who have 'chosen' abortion. To do so would be to condemn myself also. And none of us has the right to condemn even ourselves because we are not, finally, our own judges. For those who view their God as a harsh, exacting judge who demands an eye for an eye and a tooth for a tooth, this fact may hold more fear than comfort. But for those who understand something of what Calvary means, it is a liberation. There is nothing – no tragedy, no inhumanity, no betrayal – which Calvary cannot encompass, redeem and heal. And this, I hope, is what this book is finally about.

Chapter One

It was the end of November and already the cold bit hard. We set out in the dark to drive from Craignish to Loch Gilphead and the bus-stop to Glasgow. I left Craignish that morning knowing that I would not be coming back. I think David sensed it too, but neither of us said anything during that long drive apart from the safe, unimportant things that people say to guard against the pain of understanding each other.

Often on the north-west coast there is a seeping damp in the winter's cold that sinks into the bone. Then the shapes of the world lose their edges and blur into the drizzling sky. During the last few days Craignish had been like that, the colours all washed out by the icy grey water that filled the air until you breathed it in and lapped against the shore and the hills, turning sky and sea into one continuous sweep of water.

Those were the last days I spent with David in the cottage by Loch Craignish. Mostly, they were days spent struggling to understand problems whose causes were too nebulous to grasp let alone to solve, while my resentment grew until all I could feel for the man I was supposed to marry was hostility. Then, suddenly, the weather had changed. Now the air snapped in the lungs and made you catch your breath, and the light shone like crystal, bringing everything into sharp relief. It was a time for seeing clearly.

We arrived at Loch Gilphead too early to buy break-fast so we stood at the bus-stop, stamping to keep the blood from freezing, our feet making noises on the stones that cracked like shots through the quiet street. We spoke very little. The sky was milky and the new sun threw no shadows. The sea was the colour of the sky, like the white belly of a fish. The two met some-where on the horizon; you could not see where. It would be a shining-blue winter's day by mid-morning. We waited for the bus beside a stone cross, a replica of an ancient celtic monument, now in a museum in Glas-gow. David's face looked raw and there was a despera-tion in it that would have made me feel sorry for him if I had been able to.

He had tried, almost from the start of our relation-ship, to persuade me that university was a waste of time – despite his own doctorate. He usually sulked when I left him to go back to lectures and tutorials, as though these were rival lovers. At first it had amused and then irritated and frustrated me. This time he was clearly making an effort to be pleasant, but the effort had come too late. His face was pinched with cold. If it was not only the cold, if something else caused that look of pain around his eyes and mouth, I had no intention of allowing him to tell me what it was. I wanted nothing from him, certainly not those words of a for-ever-and-always love which, though he offered it as if it were a gift, demanded sole ownership in return. This last time together was something to be endured, a time which must pass without incident until I was safely on the bus to Glasgow. I assumed an air of normality with which I prevented any soul-bar-ing, any discussion – even any real contact.

We said goodbye politely, David looking for words that I would not let him find. It was not that I was afraid he would dissuade me if I gave him the chance, at least not from going back to Monday's tutorials. But David had a Svengali-like personality, obsessional and powerful. If he guessed how far my feelings for him had altered he would not rest until he had persuaded me that I was confused or mistaken or had agreed to try and salvage something of our former relationship. To risk any discussion would be to risk leaving him with some kind of hold over me.

As the bus pulled away from Loch Gilphead I made myself busy with my case and tickets so that I could avoid waving, avoid meeting his eyes. I was still afraid that he would discover the truth, would read it in my face, that my only feeling for him now was a deep and bitter dislike.

The journey was one I might have enjoyed at another time. The sky was clearing and the world was polished silver under the winter sun. I liked the bumpy little roads and the bumpy little hills on either side of the roads. Apart from the residual unpleasantness of parting with David, however, I was also feeling sick. This was not a result of the bus ride. It had developed and become increasingly persistent over the past few days. I would certainly have worried about it if not for the fact that I was also experiencing a sort of numb detachment not only from everything around me but from everything that happened to me.

I was, I think, in a kind of shock. I no longer had any illusions about our relationship and all our intimacy had been based on illusion. I had realised this with growing horror, which had changed to become the dull nothingness inside. In fact, I seemed to be able to feel very little now apart from the near hatred I had developed for my onetime fiancé and the continual nausea. The two ran into each other – like paints on a wet paper making one ugly colour.

The bus stopped to let the passengers have breakfast at a small hotel whose name I have forgotten. (It is one of the features of the west-coast highlanders that comfort and ease rank high on their list of priorities and time-tables and schedules considerably lower.) I marked my escape from life with David by eating two hot meat pasties, after six months of vegetarianism! It was not merely a gesture. The thought of any non-meat food that morning made me feel ill. If I had known anything, then, about the food cravings of a pregnant woman I might have realised what was wrong with me.

It was not until some weeks later that I did find out. It was the winter break and I had gone home from university for Christmas. Not only did I still feel nauseous, but I had begun suffering from low, abdominal pains. In the time-honoured fashion of egocentric teenagers I made sure the rest of the family suffered from them too! I moaned about them but, typically, did nothing else. My mother, however, decided that if anything were seriously wrong with me it should be dealt with as quickly as possible – preferably before the new semester began – and arranged for me to see a doctor the same weekend.

He was not my local GP, but the only local doctor available on a Saturday. I was nervous, worried that perhaps something really was wrong, and besides the surgery was miles away so, all in all, I was grateful that my mother offered to drive me there. I wished afterwards that she hadn't, that I had gone alone and that she had not been there during the dreadful consultation.

'What was the date of your last period?'

A routine question, but it was one I couldn't answer

immediately. It had been October, more than two months previously. The implication of this had not occurred to me until now.

'And is it possible that you might have become pregnant after this time?'

It was.

'Well, I can't say with absolute certainty, of course, without doing an examination, and you should hand in a sample of urine for testing as soon as possible, but the strong probability is that you are pregnant.'

Why hadn't I realised? I'd had two irregular periods and then none for two months. I had just assumed that my cycle was 'settling down' – or something. What an idiot! If I could have been alone at that moment perhaps I might have found some equilibrium with which to cope in the months that followed, or perhaps that is wishful thinking. From then on, however, there seemed always to be too many people around, always other people being affected by my 'tragedy', or anxious to help in the crisis.

My mother's face was frozen with the effort not to register her dismay; not to appear shocked or hurt in case I felt rejected by her. She would have preferred to be alone too right then. She had her own private grief; for her own baby who would have to grow up so quickly now with a child to look after; for the baby I was carrying who would grow up without its father – and for herself. It was not the pain of imagining she felt, but that of knowledge. A widow at twenty-eight, with three young children, she had raised us alone for thirteen years. I had seen her crying more than once while we were still young, from loneliness and fear and from her sense of inadequacy in the face of what she felt to be an immense responsibility.

She tried to remain impassive as the doctor spoke. My mother does a rotten job of disguising her feelings.

13

She always has done. The disguises she wears are transparent; I even know how she assumes those necessary masks to her soul which she wears so badly. 'Right, now, this is me being impassive,' she tells herself, and her impassivity is taut and desperate. Looking back at her now, sitting in that small green and white room in our shared past, I smile. Back there, the nineteen-year-old I was just wished that she were not there or that her pain did not touch me, did not even communicate itself.

The doctor was explaining the options, and I had missed half of what he had said. My own thoughts seemed to have been amplified to the point of making it difficult to hear anything else.

He's trying to be brisk. It's his way of being kind. He's right, too, it does help. Sympathy would kill me.

'If you want a termination,' he said, 'it ought to be done as soon as possible...'

What's a termination?

'...relatively simple operation...'

Oh, an abortion.

'You would go in on a Friday and be home the following Sunday.'

Oh, I wish it would just go away like that, like going to sleep and waking up to find it was only a bad dream, not really happening at all.

'If that's what you wanted I could arrange it for you...'

'Oh no!'

My mother had spoken, not I. But she was right. I didn't yet believe in the child inside me, but if there were one there I couldn't just snuff it out. You don't subject human beings to pest control. I was perfectly clear about that intellectually. The problem was I didn't *feel* like that. I felt as if I was in someone else's nightmare and I wanted it to stop.

'No,' I said finally, 'I don't want an abortion.'

A few days later my own GP confirmed the pregnancy. She had carried out a quick examination and found that I was eight or nine weeks pregnant. Still the growing child I was carrying was only an idea and one in which I did not yet believe. Perhaps this was because I did not want to believe in it, and perhaps it was also because I was already feeling numb and removed from everything about me. Now this feeling increased.

Emotionally I needed time to forgive myself and David for the travesty of love which had taken place between us. The discovery of my pregnancy meant that much as I wanted to I could not distance myself from that relationship. In fact, the child could only involve me in a further commitment to a man I could no longer even like.

It took a few days before I could bring myself to phone David and tell him that I was pregnant. It was no great surprise to him. He had thought I might be, he said. He had recognised the symptoms. He had no illusions that I might now marry him. I had written him a letter after our last meeting in November, saying that I did not want to see him again, that I thought he was so self-absorbed that he was incapable of the unselfishness or the generosity needed to make a relationship work. It was a brutal letter.

Now he simply wanted to know what I intended to do about the baby. I told him that I didn't yet know whether I would keep the child or have him or her adopted. The thought of adoption, a child of his whom he would never see or know, hurt him badly. His response to the pain was what I would have expected. Better to have an abortion than to do that to him. I hung up on him. I was churning inside, but did not shout or cry. I switched the feelings off, became a little more numb, and the world just seemed a little uglier.

Physically I still felt very sick, and to make matters worse my senses seemed to have become more acute. Strong smells were overpowering and could send me rushing for the nearest sink or lavatory; strong tastes made my stomach heave. The cold and dark of a rainy December seemed animate and vicious. As the invasion of a hostile world continued, so did my withdrawal.

Fear wears a multitude of shapes and faces. The wide-eyed terror of the movie screen is only one of them. Refusal to face or to deal with something is a much more common and much less obvious one. Someone you think of as a stoic, someone who appears calm and self-contained in the face of a terrible crisis, may in fact be refusing to deal with reality at all. She is not 'rising above' her feelings. She is avoiding what she is afraid is too terrible to bear, by refusing to feel anything at all. She makes a sort of zombie of herself while seeming normal, under the circumstances, to those around her. I was one of these.

A pregnant woman who does not want her pregnancy is very often, indeed probably more often than not, afraid. I am convinced that fear is by far the commonest motive for abortion, and fear is a very bad reason for doing anything. It is almost always a lie, a voice that whispers in secret, 'You can't cope with that; you aren't able.'

It whispers many other things to the pregnant woman who is alone. It tells her that when the child is born she will no longer be desirable; that she will lose the chance to make something of her life; that she will be trapped in poverty and loneliness; that she cannot love the child of a man whom she does not love. It whispers other things too, more subtle and less easy to

16

define. It tells her that she will never be the same again if she has this baby. It does not tell her that she is already altered by pregnancy beyond any going back. It tells her that she is paying the price for her stupidity or her sin. It will twist the child's true shape, which is life's act of faith in her, into the shape of judgement and condemnation.

Who will she name these fears to? Often not even to herself. They are ugly, shameful fears that expose her weakness. If there is someone she can talk to who understands them and can name them for her, two things may be achieved. The first is that if she has withdrawn to escape the situation, she may come out of her emotional paralysis and start to deal with her own feelings. The second is that the lie can be given to those subjective horrors which, because they are so frightening, have all the force of inexorable facts.

She is strong enough to go through this pregnancy. Literally millions of women have been in the same position and have coped very well. Her life will not come to an end and certainly need not be ruined. With a little help there is nothing she cannot do. If she can be helped to forgive the child's father, and perhaps herself, then a very common problem, rejection of the child because of its father, is resolved. She can be helped to see that a child is not a simple compound of two people, but the child of generations of people of whom its father and mother are just two in the long line of descent. Most of all she can and should be helped to see that however wrong or stupid the act that conceived her child, its presence is not a punishment. It is an affirmation of her femininity; the signal of life's belief in her.

Acknowledging her fears, challenging and defeating them, allows a woman to look at her pregnancy without mentally backing away in horror. The nightmare-vision comes into a truer perspective. This in turn means that she can begin to relate to the child that she is carrying. The barriers created by fear can begin to come down.

There was, unfortunately, no one who could help me to overcome my hatred of David, my dread of the lies whispered by fear, my complete lack of self-respect. This was not because I was alone or unloved, but because there was no one close to me who had any idea of the secret nightmare which I was enduring. To make matters worse my beloved family cosseted me as if I were the victim of some natural disaster, unwittingly putting the finishing touches to the picture of tragedy which was all I could see of my pregnancy.

Within a week or two of the first suggestion that I might be pregnant, another incident occurred which pushed me further into the shadowland I now moved in.

Chapter Two

I decided very quickly, too quickly perhaps, that I would have the child adopted when he or she was born. My GP asked me to go and discuss this with her because she was connected with a church adoption agency and would be able to make the necessary arrangements. I went. Even now I do not know if the doctor misrepresented the philosophy of the agency, or if their emphasis was really so concentrated on the unborn child and his adoptive parents that the natural mother barely counted as a human being.

I do not recall that interview clearly. Of all the major incidents during my pregnancy that one is still so painful that when I do try to remember the details, some part of me pushes them away. Briefly, however, I was told that one week after the birth my baby would be collected by someone from the adoption agency. I could be told nothing whatever about the adoptive parents and could not know, nor stipulate in any way, the sort of home my child would grow up in.

Something of my own maternity must have survived my panic and withdrawal from the situation because I questioned this. It seemed to me that to hand my child over to a stranger, to be given to other strangers, with whom I had had no contact and about whom I had no information of any kind to reassure me, was something like throwing the child over the edge of an abyss. In response to this I was told that I had no rights whatsoever in the matter. The adoption agency was providing a service which would relieve me of my responsibility. In turn they had to consider the future welfare of the adoptive parents and the child.

That at least was the essence of what the doctor said. Unspoken was the clear message: 'You have got yourself into this mess. We will get you out of it, but you cannot expect to dictate the terms. You should have thought of this before you acted irresponsibly.'

The pain tightened inside like the coils of a constrictor that lay wound around my stomach. As if my emotional 'circulation' were being cut off, the cold, dead feeling increased. I was to incubate the pregnancy, that was all. No further counselling or discussion was offered. Believing that I had no other choice, I agreed to the agency's terms and the adoption procedure was put in motion.

That final, callous severance of mother from child may have been the child's death warrant. Officialdom had certified my total lack of interest in, concern for, or involvement in the future life of my child. The demand that I voluntarily surrender any stake whatever in the ordinary feelings and interests of motherhood ended any possibility of relating normally to him or her before it was too late.

In later years when I debated abortion in front of the usual polarisation of pro- and anti-abortionists, and argued for adoption as an alternative, I was accused, more than once, of reducing women to the status of incubators for other people. The irony of the accusation, though it struck me deeply, did not hurt. I understood the feelings behind it. What my accusers objected to was precisely what had happened to me. In a peculiar way, it was me they were defending!

It is not adoption itself which is offensive. Far from it. It is the possibility which it creates of rendering a child into a commodity and his mother into the producer of a commodity. These days, thank God, adoption services are far more loving, sensible and sensitive towards the mother's needs and emotions. They are usually only too aware that they are dealing with people's lives and not with commodities or the producers thereof! As a rule they appreciate the sacrifice a woman makes when she gives her child to others to belong and to grow up with. They realise that she must retain the right to have some say as to the sort of home her child will grow up in; that she must be able to like and approve of the people who will take her place as the child's parents.

Yet I often wonder how many mothers have been brutalised by well-meaning adoption agencies. How many times have those concerned for the child and prospective parents effectively dismissed the needs and feelings of the natural mother? They have insulted her, regarding her principally as a danger, liable to behave irresponsibly, and incapable even of sharing in the decision-making concerning the future of her child. They have violated her motherhood by refusing to allow her the certainty she needs that the baby will be properly loved and cared for by parents whom she trusts. And how many women have been so hurt by the punitive manner in which adoption has been presented, that they have chosen abortion instead? However deserving of protection and concern the child and his adoptive parents are, there is no excuse for minimalising a woman's relationship with her baby.

Appalled by the inhumanity of the adoption procedure, and as unaware as I that other adoption agencies might do things differently, my mother suggested that

I marry David, have the baby, then divorce him and claim maintenance. The marriage would not in fact have been necessary in order to have obtained maintenance. David was very wealthy and would have made provisions for his child without being forced to do so either by a divorce court or a paternity suit. I did not want anything from him, however, and was not prepared to accept the financial help which he could easily and would readily have given.

If I had not been so hostile that I was determined to have no contact with him whatsoever, I might have considered keeping the baby. As it was, I knew that I would have to struggle to provide the basics for the child myself and that it would have been impossible to pay for the nursery care which would allow me to continue my degree. I telephoned David and told him that I intended to have the baby adopted. I did not see or speak to him again for almost five years.

Christmas was dreadful. My mother, brother, sister and grandparents were all present and all knew that I was pregnant. They tried not to refer to the fact in any way and I wasn't sure whether they were embarrassed about it, whether they did not want to embarrass me by mentioning it, or both. What should have been a time of celebration became an ordeal for everyone. They were all walking on eggshells whenever I was present, which made me more depressed and irritable still. That in turn made life more unpleasant for everyone. Inevitably the tension occasionally became too great and something more like war than family arguments broke out between us. It must have been a relief when I went back to university at the end of the holiday.

By the time the new term began all the arrangements for the birth of the baby had been made. I was to go into a hospital in Aberdeen, where a relative worked as a gynaecologist, for the birth. I would be given an epidural – an injection which blocks off all feeling from the waist down – so that I would not experience any pain during labour. The baby would then be collected from the hospital by the adoption agency one week later. I do not remember anyone telling me then that legally I could change my mind about the adoption right up to the moment when the child was collected.

It was a cold, grey January. Too cold for real snow. The little that fell lay thin and dirty on the ground before dissolving. With only a few days to go before term started, I realised that I couldn't stay any longer in the flat which I had been sharing, with two others, for most of the previous term. My bedroom was damp and ugly. There was a permanent odour of stale food from the kitchen which combined with the damp to create a peculiar and revolting smell. The paint on the walls was garish: purple in one room, bright green in another. My 'digs in town' had seemed Bohemian and adult when I moved in. Now they only seemed squalid and smelly, and I was desperate to get out of them.

Having moved off campus during my first term I had given up my entitlement to live in university halls for the first year. Not unreasonably, I had to give the university Accommodation Officer special reasons for allowing me to move back again. I did. The disclosure of my pregnancy produced the usual effect of hastily disguised shock and, a welcome side-effect this time, a speedy accession to my request. I moved the following day into one of the little white cells, as the students very aptly described their rooms in the halls of residence.

Mostly the students minimised the 'cell' effect of their white, breeze-block rooms by covering the walls in posters, and importing coloured rugs, ornaments, flowers and so on. When I had first been given one of these rooms at the beginning of the year, I had done the same. Now I left it bare. The blank anonymity of

23

those white walls, if not actually comforting, at least did not impose, and left me in a kind of peace. The friends who occasionally called round found it unpleasant, like a waiting room, and would tactfully suggest improvements. I made no changes. I liked it precisely because it was anonymous. I could come and go, leaving no trace of myself. And anyone who came in would find no clue to the person who lived there.

I hated the cold even more than usual. I went to tutorials and the odd lecture, wrote essays and skipped through the prescribed books. Much of my time was spent in the library which, like my room, was always warm and anonymous. I watched my fellow students from a distance, with no inclination to try to bridge the gap I felt between us.

In the months before I had found myself pregnant I had enjoyed being a part of student life. Being one of the crowd was reassuring as well as fun. The norms of behaviour, however, were vicious. Most of my friends and acquaintances aspired to the all-important ideal of sophistication. Sharp, witty and cruel in the speech they affected, 'liberal' in morals, fashionable in politics, they hid a terrible loneliness behind their assumed personas. It was part of the price you paid for being sophisticated. Considering that those of us who went to university were supposed to be the brightest of our generation, we were extraordinarily stupid!

I no longer qualified, nor was I anxious now, to join the crowd whose social activities consisted mainly of parties and gatherings at the pub-cum-disco, where the chief interest was playing romantic roundabouts. Actually 'romantic' is not a good description since the word implies such things as poetry, tenderness and love. In retrospect there was little, if anything, of these in the frantic partner-hunting that went on in the background of almost all social events at university.

And once successfully hunted, a partner almost automatically became a lover. Sex began these usually short-lived relationships. It did not develop along the way and it certainly wasn't the final expression of a permanent commitment. A significant number of female students needed treatment for depression and neurosis, almost all of these because of on-campus relationships. Others passed by another automatic process through the medical centre to have abortions at the local hospital.

Pregnancy was something which 'wasn't done'. This was largely because it made you undesirable as a partner and so reduced your social rating. (You couldn't be sophisticated and pregnant!) Then it required a certain amount of unselfish support from friends, something that tended to be in short supply in our egocentric, student world. Pregnancy was an embarrassment, too, inasmuch as it underlined the fact that casual sexual relationships might not be as harmless as we liked to think. All in all I now represented a problem which made it difficult for most of those in my social circle to behave normally towards me. Not surprisingly, I went home as often as possible – from Thursday night to Monday morning if I could manage it.

Not only did I see my family at weekends, but I could spend time with the only people who didn't treat me either as a walking tragedy or a social pariah! I had four friends, Ian, Robbie, Alan and Rosie, with whom I had been part of a close little group since secondary school. We were comfortable with and loyal to each other. They had decided that there was very little they could do to help me except look after me through the pregnancy and ensure that I didn't become depressed, isolated or house-bound. This caretaking involved such rituals as our going out in the evenings to a quiet pub where someone, having generously bought me a gin and tonic, would suddenly realise that I shouldn't be drinking alcohol at all and substitute it with some far less attractive soft drink!

Robbie had recently been 'dumped' by his first serious girlfriend. We all knew it was a major tragedy. We had no doubts about how much he loved her. He was thus being looked after too, although not having to limit his intake of alcohol, he spent as much time as he possibly could getting so drunk that he couldn't remember who or where he was. To my astonishment one evening, when he was less drunk than usual, he leaned over, kissed me and asked me to go out with him. The fact that I was pregnant apparently only mattered to him in so far as it might make me unwilling to consider the idea. He had been worried about that, he said. (And true or not it was excellent psychology!) What did matter was that we were already friends, we liked and cared about each other and right then we both needed comfort and affection. By the end of the night the two 'waifs' of the party were evidently a couple, much to the relief of our friends for whom it was an answer to prayer. The comfort they had tried and failed to give us both, we could give one another.

From then on Robbie drank less and I did more of the silly, happy things that teenagers enjoy. Ian persuaded his father to lend him his Mercedes. He drove like a maniac, but none of us minded at all. We thought nothing could happen to us. (Which only goes to show that you can't always trust quiet, sensible sons to be quiet, sensible drivers!) We swapped the latest records and went to the Genesis concert in Glasgow. We went for beach barbecues consisting of sausages 'removed' from our mothers' freezers, and beer 'appropriated' from the boys' fathers. I was on coca-cola most of the time, watched by my benign keepers to make sure that I obeyed the laws of pregnancy! Occasionally I was allowed the odd lager, which tasted particularly good with a sausage that was too hot, eaten on a beach that was too cold.

I blamed alcohol for the reoccurrence of the abdominal pain which had sent me to the doctor in the first place. I knew that alcohol should be avoided during pregnancy and wondered if perhaps a single drink could do some unimaginable harm. In fact I drank very little indeed, certainly too little to do any serious damage. The real cause of the pain had never been investigated. It appeared to have been attributed simply to the fact that I was pregnant, though I cannot imagine why. I was now some twelve weeks pregnant. It wasn't severe, but there was something frightening about that pain, although I couldn't have explained why. I went back to my GP.

She was serious as she examined me and pointed out something which I had not previously noticed. My breasts, enlarged by pregnancy at the time when she had first examined me, had altered. The tenderness to the touch and the swollen appearance of pregnancy were gone. Instead they seemed flabby and shapeless. When she had completed her examination she was silent for a few moments. The size of my womb was too small for the stage the pregnancy had reached. In her opinion, she said, the child had died. She was wrong, in fact, but this was not discovered for some weeks. In the meantime she sent me to the nearest hospital for tests. She added: 'I think you had better forget about this pregnancy. Get on with your life and try to put the whole thing behind you if you can.'

I left the surgery telling myself that it was all over, the bad dream was finished. I couldn't make myself believe it, however. With one of those peculiar predictive certainties which most of us experience at some time or other, I knew that the worst was only just beginning.

Chapter Three

I was sent to the nearest hospital a few days later and placed under observation in a side ward in the maternity wing. From my room I could hear the sounds of new-born babies and, from time to time, their mothers talking happily in the hospital corridor.

I had been told to forget about my own pregnancy, but whether I could really do so or not depended on the outcome of tests to determine whether the child was still alive or had died in the womb, as my GP believed. I desperately wanted the whole thing to be over, but if it were not, if I was to give birth to a child whom I would hand over to strangers, to be separated thereafter both from the child and, by an eternity of experience, from all the friends of my own age, then I wanted to know as quickly as possible.

The necessary tests were not carried out. Instead, I was left alone in a small room where, for the first day, I saw only the auxiliaries who brought meals or tea and coffee, and two nurses. The first nurse was in her late fifties, I suppose. She spoke to me while taking my pulse, temperature and so on, as if I were a mentally deficient child and explained, with the magical, tell-at-a-glance wisdom of experience and the certainty of the very unimaginative, that I was fine. In a few weeks, she said, I would have "a big round bump" and after that a baby. After she had left I burst into tears.

The second nurse was nearer my own age. As she left she turned and said: 'You don't want this baby, do you?'

I don't remember what I replied, something about wanting to know whether I was going to have a child at all and not knowing what to feel in the meantime. But the reply hardly mattered as she was already leaving. By the next morning fear and isolation had tuned my nerves until I felt as taut as a piano-wire. I lay quietly until visiting time, but by then something had happened which had left me with only a veneer of emotional control.

In the afternoon the consultant gynaecologist, whom I will call Mr Brown, had visited. He had been doing his rounds with a group of male medical students. They were not much older than I. In fact several of my friends were studying medicine, probably at the same university. Their arrival made me a little uneasy. I realised that the consultant would want to examine me, but I had never become used to undressing for male doctors, let alone students of my own age. I prepared to try to hide my embarrassment as Mr Brown asked my permission to examine me in the presence of the medical students. Embarrassment became panic, however, when it turned out that Mr Brown wanted to perform a vaginal examination under the scrutiny of this band of young men in order to instruct them. Worse, he wanted them to examine me in the same manner.

It is true that he had only made a request – "I would like these students to examine you please...", but he adopted a tone of voice which made it sound like an announcement – as though either I had no choice or he had no doubt about my agreeing.

I was nineteen and had only undergone an internal examination twice before – and then by a woman doc-

29

tor. Even so I had found it invasive and extremely unpleasant. The consultant had explained that these medical students were in need of practical experience and in doing so he had admitted that they were unused to the procedure. Several of them showed obvious embarrassment and I felt as though I had been asked to agree to something pornographic, something closely resembling rape.

Although I was used to doing as I was told by professional medics, this time I was more afraid of the violation he intended than of disobeying him. I asked, in a very small voice, whether I could refuse. The consultant was furious. I had the right to refuse of course, he said, but he wanted to know how doctors were expected to learn their profession if women like myself insisted on being such prudes.

By this time I could barely speak, but the assault (for that is how I perceived it) to which he intended to subject me was more than I could bear.

'Then I refuse,' I said.

He left without another word and the students, looking as relieved as I felt, followed him. It still seems bizarre to me that Mr Brown proposed to teach them how to conduct such an intimate examination by using a traumatised, pregnant girl. He must have been fully aware that they were too young to have acquired his own professional disinterest and too inexperienced to have overcome their sexual feelings. If his intention was to make them overcome this handicap by throwing them in at the deep end, which seems the likeliest explanation, then he was profoundly callous or at best profoundly indifferent to the feelings and the dignity of his patient.

Obviously performing a successful balancing act between professional objectivity and callousness cannot be easy. It is, however, more important than it might seem, especially as it affects the practice of abortion. Callousness is easily acquired and easily taught and with it comes the degradation, the dehumanising of those who are under medical supervision. One thing is certain: only by depersonalising a mother into a mere patient and her unborn child into 'foetal tissue' could anyone knowingly destroy the foetus in utero and violate the relationship between mother and child.

We accept medical callousness without differentiating it from objectivity – and we ought not to. It brutalises our medical profession and it brutalises those in their care. The depersonalising of the patient can have a profound effect on a pregnant woman, encouraging her to perceive herself as a medical case with a medical problem rather than as a mother who has problems. It may even become the mental shield which allows her to go through with an abortion she would not otherwise have had.

Indeed, some abortion counsellors strive to maintain an approach with their clients – women seeking abortion – that is as clinical and impersonal as possible for this very reason. They help to shield her mind from the human realities of her situation by substituting a clinical version. They help her to avoid the terrible emotions she might otherwise be feeling – emotions that will only 'cloud her judgement'. Yet these very emotions are what make her human.

In other circumstances any woman would automatically reject being treated in this way, as though her feelings did not exist, but when she is seeking an abortion I know for a fact that she will be profoundly grateful for it. Does this make it a good thing for some women? We should ask instead what it is about abortion that it so often requires a sense of degradation, emotional numbness and dehumanisation in a woman before she can go ahead with it.

After Mr Brown and his group of students had left, I lay silent until visiting time, but as soon as my mother appeared I became almost hysterical so that I could not make her understand what had happened. When she was unable to find out what was wrong and unable to stop me crying she became concerned about the danger of my miscarrying simply from stress. Even so, she did not seriously consider taking me home – which I kept begging her to do – until she realised that no tests had been done and that I did not believe any would be done. She made enquiries to the sister on duty who checked my medical notes. There were no tests scheduled; no blood tests, no urine tests, no ultra-sound scan. I was to be kept in hospital for a week or so for observation only. My normally docile mother exploded: 'But that's useless! She was admitted for tests. Are you saying that you have no intention of doing them?'

The sister raised her eyebrows. 'She was admitted at the request of her GP. We have no plans to carry out any tests.'

'Then I don't think she ought to remain here.'

My mother argued that I was in a far worse state than I had been when I had come into hospital and there seemed to be no pressing reason for me to stay. On the other hand there were very good reasons why I should not become any more upset than I already was. She decided to take me home. I signed myself out, which means that I signed a form saying that I had discharged myself from hospital against medical advice and that I would not hold the hospital responsible if I were to suffer any harm as a result.

I did not come to any harm – well, no more harm than had already been done by the twenty-four hours I had spent in hospital. Neither did I find out what, if anything, was wrong with the pregnancy. The GP who had arranged the adoption greeted me at the next appointment with a cold anger for having discharged myself. It seemed that the consultant, 'Mr Brown', had given her a tongue lashing for having referred me to him in the first place and had complained of my non-co-operation. She did not ask me what had happened or why I had signed myself out of the hospital. Before I left, however, she agreed to refer me to a private specialist. I was given an appointment with him the following week.

At this time I was living what amounted to a double life. Back at university I talked very little about the pregnancy. My stomach was still very flat so nobody could have guessed I was pregnant and in fact only a handful knew about it. I was still seeing Robbie, and occasionally he would bring the gang (Ian, Alan and Rosie) over to see me at the halls of residence. We never mentioned my 'condition' and they continued to treat me exactly as they had done in the past. After their initial concern, they found it easiest to behave as though nothing had happened – there was nothing to see, after all! – and I was glad to be able to pretend that things were just as they always had been. When I had to face pity or awkwardness or condemnation, then I had to face reality. Otherwise I shut out the truth as far as I possibly could.

I was not, therefore, looking forward to my appointment with the specialist, from whom the best I could hope for was that he would be a competent technician. In my experience so far, humanity or compassion were not qualities to be found among medics!

Mr Chalmers was probably in his late fifties, grey-haired and with a gentle voice and manner. To my astonishment he treated me with kindness. He had read my case notes, of course, and asked me to tell him what had been happening over the past weeks. When I had finished my brief and not very detailed account he shook his head and said, 'Poor old girl. You have had a time of it, haven't you?'

He examined me, apologising first for the fact that it wasn't a particularly nice experience to undergo. I have remained grateful to him ever since for treating me with such humanity. When the examination was over he said exactly what the GP had said only a few weeks before. I was to try to forget about the pregnancy and pick up the pieces of my life. My pregnancy was now some fifteen weeks' gestation and my womb, he explained, should have been the size of a grapefruit (he made the shape with the fingers of two hands). Instead, it was the normal size for an eleven to twelve week pregnancy. He was going to refer me to an Edinburgh hospital for an ultrasound scan, but he had very little doubt that it would confirm his diagnosis that the child had died in the womb.

If, instead, he had confirmed that the pregnancy was quite normal, I think that I might have begun to accept it, accept the child I was carrying and my new and terrifying identity as a mother. This doctor gave the impression that he understood, and that he cared how I felt. It is difficult to explain exactly what that meant. Until then I had felt as if I were a walking tragedy to my family, a charity case to my GP and the adoption society, a number to the hospital and an inconvenience to all.

Sympathy and pity are not the same thing. The first can be given with respect, the second demeans the person it is directed towards. Sympathy involves trying to put yourself in another's shoes, allowing yourself to realise how you would feel in the same situation – sharing another's pain to some small extent. Pity only wonders what the pain the other is suffering would be like. It knows it would be awful, but it could not consider

34

such pain happening to itself. Pity contains an unspoken sense of superiority or profound difference from the person towards whom it is directed. This doctor offered his sympathy without pity and allowed me dignity.

The importance of this cannot be underestimated. I believe that very often it is not pregnancy that a woman cannot accept, but herself, or the image of herself which society has created for the single mothers of 'unplanned' children. It is an image which pity reinforces quite as much as condemnation. I know that in my own case the need for self-esteem and the fear of being classed as 'one of those women' was a crucial factor. I needed to be treated in a way that would rebuild the self-respect which I had lost, but because I did not believe I deserved such acceptance I neither expected nor looked for it.

Those friends who had been most supportive had simply behaved as if my pregnancy didn't exist. They had allowed me to function as myself – the self I had been before the pregnancy. What I needed most of all, though, was to be treated as normal *and* pregnant. I needed to talk about what I was going through without feeling like a freak or a criminal. I felt that I deserved whatever was happening to me and I didn't blame anyone for pitying or for patronising me but, naturally, I didn't want to endure either. So I tried to appear as normal as possible, to give no one any reason to say: 'Poor soul, wouldn't it be awful to be like that?' or: 'Well, if she's having a bad time she only has herself to blame!'

And the more calm and normal I appeared, the less obvious my real and terrible need was. In one sense I was right, I did deserve what I was suffering because I had consciously entered into a sexual relationship of which pregnancy is the natural consequence. I realise

35

now, however, that what I deserved was actually irrelevant. After all, if any of us deserved acceptance we would not need it in the first place! Since none of us is wholly admirable and since no one escapes from the often agonising consequences of his own mistakes, we all require the love and acceptance of others and we are all required to support those in distress without judgement. For those who receive it, love is a privilege; for those who give it, it is a duty.

I am sure that the question of self-esteem is equally important for any woman in the same position because the worse your self-image is, the less you believe yourself capable of doing what you know to be right, and the less important it is to do it. That is how fear becomes a more important factor in decision making than your own integrity.

When the consultation was finished, Mr Chalmers called my mother, who was waiting outside, into his surgery. He told her that the pregnancy was finished and that it was important that I get on with my life as normally as possible. Before he could explain what would happen in the next few weeks she had interrupted: 'Do you mean that the baby is dead?'

I winced. There was an unintentional brutality in the words. It was contained, I think, in her overriding concern for the unborn child which had caused her to enquire after his or her wellbeing before that of her daughter; contained in her fear that Mr Chalmers had only dismissed the pregnancy because of possible handicap, a fear which made it more important to clarify the truth than to save my feelings. I understood her position, but I resented it. It was my place to establish the facts, not hers. As my mother I felt she should have been concerned enough about my state of mind to speak tactfully. I felt she should have understood that the doctor was not baldly stating a truth he had already broken to me as gently as possible, because he felt that I had already been traumatised. I resented the fact that while he had intuitively recognised the extent of that trauma she evidently had not.

He answered her by restating that the pregnancy was finished and, I think, by saying that he would prefer not to use the language she had employed. I should have been more thoughtful of her distress. I should have cared that he was dismissing her feelings, but instead I was grateful to him for reacting to her question with a resentment that answered my own. He had felt the sting in her words and knew that they had hurt me.

I know that she suspected him of using euphemistic language to obscure the humanity of my child. On the way home she asked repeatedly whether I was sure that he had said the child had actually died. I think we had a row about it. In any case, I could not make her understand that he had chosen his words only to obscure the brutality of the facts and not to obscure the facts themselves.

She could not understand his kindness because she didn't begin to understand my plight. She knew that mothers always loved their children. She was sure that unless there was something wrong with her, the maternal instinct made every mother want her child. Rejection and fear of an unborn child was an alien, unimaginable thing. So, therefore, was the guilt which is the flip side of that coin. To her, grief for a dead child was a simple thing. To me it presented a network of complicated emotions, not least of which was the sense of inadequacy – perhaps even inhumanity – at my inability to love.

A few days later I was admitted to hospital for a scan. A nurse poured warm oil over my abdomen and slowly pushed the end of some electrical apparatus over it. An

37

image came up on the screen at my feet. This time the elderly specialist, who stared intently at the fuzz of black and green lines on the monitor, had no doubt at all.

'Well, there it is, alive, about thirteen weeks' gestation.'

'Alive? Are you sure?' I demanded.

'Perfectly. Look for yourself. There! You can see the heart beating.'

I couldn't make out anything distinct at all, but there was a rhythmic pulse near the middle of the picture. I didn't understand how the dates could have been so far out. My GP had found an eight to nine week gestation at the beginning of December. I should now be sixteen weeks pregnant, or thereabouts. A mistake, said the specialist, on the part of my GP. I left the hospital in a daze. It just wasn't fair. I'd had enough. I shouldn't have to go through any more – or so I told myself. It wasn't any use me trying to think about the child. I couldn't. When I left the hospital I went for a long walk.

On my last day at Craignish, in November, I had taken another long walk, across the near shore of the loch. The land was grey-brown in that season. I thought it simply desolate. I did not see the gold of the turning bracken which shot it through. I moved up to the headland, watching the swans on the water. The Craignish swans arrive each year from who knows where to spend the winter on the loch. They are wonderful birds and the sight of about sixty of them together was one I never got used to. Seals were playing off the headland, from which you can see the island of Jura on a clear day, and the rooks called from their high nests in the trees behind the castle. A mist came down suddenly and it all disappeared into the cloud, apart from the sad harsh voices of the rooks. Thirty pairs of swans moved without apparent effort across the still water, ghost-like through the film of grey.

Once before, on an early autumn evening, I had stood on the same headland watching the stars whiten and the last pink light of the sun catching the snow on the mountains of far-away Jura. Then I had thought that the beauty of the place had a kind of magic about it. Now I had forgotten that its beauty had ever existed or that I had ever known it. I was due to leave the next morning and looked forward to doing so as if making my escape from prison. I had no love left for the place where I had conceived my, as yet unknown of, child nor for his father. I returned to the cottage to finish packing. And I remember the sound of the water lapping sadly in the rushes only yards from my bedroom window.

It was like that with the child. From the time that my pregnancy was confirmed I seemed to be moving in a grey fog and the landscape of my world looked wholly bleak. I heard from a distance the call of the child's life on my love and protection; a call that would only draw me back to memories I wanted to escape. I was unaware of the mysterious beauty of motherhood, although it was there whether I knew it or not. When you look at a thing, what you see very often depends on the climate of your feelings at the time. How we feel is obviously apt to change dramatically with the passage of time, so we cannot decide what is real and true only on the basis of how we feel at a particular time. But we have become used to subjectivising reality, to assuming that it is in fact the way we feel or perceive it to be at any given moment. Acting on the basis of 'facts' which change as our moods and our perspectives change is now so acceptable that very often a doctor will refer a woman for an abortion simply on the basis of her state of mind at that time.

And the truth was that at that time I felt no more than

a child myself – and a very unhappy one at that. I was panicking, sure that I couldn't cope. I could think of no one I could talk to who would understand my feelings, no one I felt able to lean on. There was Mr Chalmers, of course, but he was a doctor not an agony aunt and besides, he was a private consultant and his time cost money. I had only my own counsel to rely on and all that I wanted was some way out of the bleakness I was living in.

I finished my walk and caught the train home. By the time I arrived I had decided that getting out was exactly what I was going to do. I did telephone Mr Chalmers then to inform him that I had decided I wanted a termination. I was not going to go through with the pregnancy. He had heard from the hospital that the child was still alive but several weeks younger than had been estimated. He sounded reluctant to refer me for an abortion, but he didn't actually raise any objections or try to dissuade me. He didn't ask me whether I wanted to go and talk to him about it nor suggest any agency where I could go for counselling and advice. He said he would sign the papers and that I would be sent an appointment from the hospital. My GP, also opposed to abortion, signed the papers too. She too did not ask me if I would like to talk about it or suggest anywhere that I could go to find a sympathetic, professional ear.

I know now that there are caring organisations all over the country which befriend, love and support unhappily pregnant mothers. They provide the sort of positive, affirmative counselling that can give a woman enough self-esteem and confidence to believe that she can face the pregnancy and then do the best for her child whether that is adoption, fostering or raising the child herself. I did not discover their existence until it was too late for me and for my child.

Chapter Four

It was a grey Friday morning in February. Robbie drove me to hospital on his way to college. I had told no one else what I was about to do. Only he knew that the ultrasound scan had detected a foetal heartbeat and that I was going into hospital, not to have a dead child taken away, but to have a living child aborted. He said very little on the way. Like me he only wanted the trauma to be over and everything to be back to normal.

Memories are nebulous things and there doesn't seem to be any obvious reason why we should remember some things and forget others. I remembered for years the rain and the date (it was Friday, 23rd February), but not what the hospital building looked like. (I now know what that building looks like, but only because I went back there eight years after the abortion. And to this day I cannot remember the names or faces of one of the doctors, nurses or orderlies I spoke to in the hospital – although I remember the other patients. I remember the admission procedure. I was weighed. My blood pressure and temperature were taken. I weighed nine-and-a-half stone, more than a stone heavier than my normal weight. That surprised me. I was asked various questions about my health and history, and I sensed that the staff who dealt with me did not like doing so. I remember a sense of shame, almost embarrassment. And there was something else, perhaps a kind of warning from my own subconscious.

I was afraid of being stopped or challenged about what I was doing. If someone had walked into the ward at that moment and asked what on earth I thought I was up to and had told me to go home, I would almost certainly have done just that. Fortunately, as it seemed, the whole procedure was very clinical and detached so that whatever feelings lay beneath the surface, no messy emotions could disrupt the professional machinery which had been put into motion. Looking back it was a very strange situation. The staff on the ward seemed to avoid any mention of what went on there. There was some unspoken understanding that the word 'abortion' should never be used. If possible the whole subject was avoided, but if it couldn't be avoided then the word they used was always 'termination'. It sounded more impersonal than abortion; more like a simple, medical procedure.

I was shown to a cubicle, where I waited for the abortion to begin. The ward was at the top of the hospital building and my bed faced one of the windows. Outside, the rain had stopped and I could see across the south side of the city. There was something odd about the way the city moved, full of people doing ordinary things. For me, it was as if time had stopped and the bustling world no longer really existed. I was out of touch with my own life and the lives of the people around me.

Partly, I think, this was an extension of my withdrawal from reality – which had begun even before I had left David. There were many reasons for that withdrawal, from my dislike of the baby's father, through my own guilt and fear, to the callousness I had suffered in the past three months. Whatever the reasons though, it came down to this: I had learned how to withdraw from what was happening to me – or from the reality of what I was doing.

This sense of dislocation, of unreality, was an important factor in two ways. In the first place because it cut me off from any protective or maternal feelings and so made abortion easier. In the second place, this state of mind made it impossible for me to make choices or take decisions which weren't dictated by panic. How could I weigh up factors I could not acknowledge, or feelings I had isolated myself from? If I was intent on remaining divorced from myself, how could I know what would be good or bad, right or wrong for the person I really was? Since I very much doubt whether I am unique in this experience, this also has a bearing on the whole notion of 'the woman's choice'. It is all very well for the pro-abortion lobby to talk about the woman's right to choose, and for them to describe themselves as pro-choice. To have any meaning, a choice must be reasoned, conscious, informed and involve other possible options.

However, there was something more happening than my own withdrawal from the reality of what was taking place. From the time that I was told I might be pregnant I had persistently felt that the pregnancy might be all a fiction. I wasn't insane. Of course I knew I was pregnant and I suffered from the knowledge, but deep down I had the feeling that the whole thing simply wasn't true. I think I know the reason for this. Perhaps, because I am describing only my own experience, it only applies to me, but it is possible that other women in the same situation have experienced the same reaction and for the same reason.

Any sexual relationship, however casual, creates a

bond between two people. They may never even be aware of it – except that it becomes glaringly obvious in the light of a woman's pregnancy. The bond between the parents of the unborn child is then inescapable, at least for the woman involved. It is part of the experience of pregnancy. How can she possibly forget the man by whom she has become pregnant, or the intimacy by which the child was conceived? In fact during the early months, sometimes for even longer, the way a woman feels about her pregnancy is very often dictated by her feelings towards the father. To feel intimately bound to someone who has rejected you or whom you have rejected is profoundly disturbing. It is hardly surprising if you then reject the pregnancy also.

But there is more involved than simply rejecting the child because of the father. Pregnancy is an overwhelming, life-changing event in any woman's life. The scale of the changes and the responsibilities involved are so great that most women will willingly undergo the experience only when they are in a supportive, stable relationship. Pregnancy, obviously, expresses the intimacy out of which the child has been conceived, but not just physical intimacy. Among many other things, it is a statement of *real* intimacy, which has begun before and is much more than just love-making; intimacy which is sustained through the shared commitment and responsibility of pregnancy and childbirth. This is not my interpretation of pregnancy. This is intrinsically true. When a woman conceives, two people become parents. They may reject their child, but they are still its parents for as long as it lives. And for as long as it lives they are bound into a relationship by their identities as mother and father of that child.

And what does it mean to be one half of the mother/

44

father relationship? What does it imply except an exclusive, committed and deeply intimate relationship? When real intimacy does not exist, when the relationship has been false or meaningless, then the pregnancy itself, expressing something which has never existed, creates a sense of violation, of some distortion of the truth. Under such circumstances, the very fact of pregnancy, might seem like a lie. The father, if he chooses to, can walk away and forget about it. The pregnant woman can't. How does a woman live with a fact in which she cannot fully believe without reality itself seeming to become less real? I think that is one of the reasons why the world outside seemed to have nothing to do with me as I waited for the abortion to begin.

Later experience has suggested that I am not the only woman who has undergone abortion in this dislocated state of mind. Nor am I alone in having been offered no counselling of any kind, either pregnancy counselling or abortion counselling, to help me to come to terms with what was happening to me. In the weeks and months which led up to the abortion, not one of the professionals I had seen, including those who were anti-abortion, so much as gave me the name of a pregnancy counselling service. Out of the accumulated experiences of my pregnancy came the clear message, 'It's your problem, get on with it.'

But unwanted pregnancy isn't only the woman's problem. It is something which fundamentally affects society. Whether she has the child or not affects the character and numbers of the new generation. Whether she keeps the child or not affects the number of children available to childless couples for adoption, perhaps determines anguish or happiness for an infertile couple and affects the demand for in vitro fertilisation programmes or surrogate motherhood.

Whether she has an abortion or not affects the kind of person she will be for the rest of her life. For a few women, abortion is the beginning of a lifetime of psychiatric illness.

It would make sense, simply as an investment in a healthy society, for the government to support pregnancy counselling and to insist on pre-abortion counselling. Perhaps one reason for the absence of either is the fact that the 'respectable' face of abortion depends on its being seen simply as a medical procedure. As soon as human emotions and relationships enter the picture, the clinical facade which disguises the realities of abortion begins to disintegrate.

Before the abortion began, a young woman doctor came to examine me. As she pressed the area around my womb I winced. She went over it more carefully, as if she were looking for something and then she asked whether I had experienced any bleeding. I had, twice; the last ocassion, only being two days previously. What she told me then has remained with me ever since as a possible defence against the many-faced horrors of self-condemnation. Either I had already begun to miscarry, or the placenta of the child I was carrying had torn.

I discovered later that if the placenta tears, the child in the womb develops very slowly because he or she is deprived of the necessary food and oxygen. It also causes low abdominal pain in the mother. This would have explained the persistent pain I had experienced – as well as all the abnormalities of my pregnancy. The baby would not have been growing at the usual rate. This meant that as long as the baby's age was being estimated according to his size and as if the growth rate were normal, then the pregnancy would keep being reassessed as younger and younger. This was, of course, exactly what had happened to me.

Eventually, the ultrasound scan had shown a living child whose size indicated no more than thirteen weeks' gestation. This was at a time when I should have been some seventeen weeks into pregnancy – according to both my own reckoning and that of the GP who first examined me. Before the scan the medics I had seen had been divided in their opinion. One side considered that the child had died, the other that there was nothing wrong with the pregnancy and that there must have been some mix up over dates. After the discovery that the child was still alive, however, the only explanation which anyone offered for the size of the baby was that the estimated date of conception had been wrong. They were quite sure of this explanation, which had only one drawback. Short of a miraculous intervention, the very latest that my pregnancy could have occurred was mid-October of the previous year. I could not physically have been less than sixteen weeks pregnant. (Having no medical training to support me, my attempts to explain this were ignored as not being worth considering. Nevertheless, I did have one important qualification, namely that I was there at the time!)

If it is true in my case that the placenta had torn in early pregnancy, causing both my pains and the apparently changing age of my baby, then the implications were and are very important to me. They mean that even though I precipitated my child's death, I was not solely responsible for it. It is small comfort but comfort, nonetheless, for which I remain very grateful.

Shortly after twelve o'clock I was moved to another bed in the centre of the ward. A drip was brought into the cubicle and a syringe was inserted into a vein in my left arm. A tube from the syringe led to the drip which contained a prostaglandin – a drug which induces labour. This drug began to feed into my bloodstream.

In the bed opposite, screened as I was by curtains, there was a woman probably in her late thirties. She didn't want to have an abortion. I had heard her explain that to the doctors. She was only going ahead because she had been told that her life might depend on it and she had a young family who depended on her. They had hooked her up to the drip before me. Neither of us asked any questions about what would happen, whether it would hurt or how long it would take. We were told only that we were to expect some pain and then we were left alone.

The pain began suddenly, ferociously. Nothing I had ever experienced, nothing I had been told had prepared me for this. My body felt as though it were waging war against itself and the onslaught came in waves with the contractions. (This is nothing like the discomfort of childbirth. Later in my life I experienced a second induced labour, this time when my son was born. It certainly hurt, but that pain was mere discomfort compared with the abortion.) Outside the hospital windows it grew dark early. The hospital ward was lit, of course, but I remember only the colour of the night outside – a blackness punctuated by crimson, the colour of the pain which had grasped my whole body. Every so often a nurse came and administered an injection. It was supposed to provide pain-relief, but it only made me terribly sleepy and gradually the pain became the chief feature of a nightmare I no longer understood. I was in the claws of some monster that was tearing at my innards and the pain came in waves as the monster's claws clenched and unclenched. The world became red and black and I lost track of time.

At just after ten o'clock in the evening it stopped as suddenly as it had begun. I felt something pass out of my body, something small and warm. I pressed the buzzer to call the nurse and lay still, afraid to look. I was afraid, I suppose, that what I would see would twist the clinical facts into the shape of a human child. He would not look like some organ from my own body. He would be a separate, self-contained entity, but more a part of me; much, much more to me than an appendix or a kidney or a liver. Perhaps he was still suffering, perhaps already dead – and by my choosing. Better not to look and then I would never know for certain. I could go on believing the clinical version that I had been pregnant and then simply wasn't pregnant any more; neat, no messy edges, no mystery of life and death, no bond of love to establish or break, just clinical facts.

It doesn't work like that, though. The effort to force abortion to hold that one, neutral face is not only futile, it can lead to madness. I did not know that at the time. But I found out.

The nurse came quickly, calling an orderly to help her. She had been on duty for eight of the ten hours in which I was in labour. She was brisk throughout, impersonal to the point of callousness, but I remember the expression of distaste on her face at that moment. I think now that her manner must have been a defence against the fact of her involvement. This was not, after all, a private clinic. She had not volunteered to be involved with abortion. In all likelihood she never would have been had not a higher power decreed that induced abortion had become part of medical 'treatment'. She gave me an injection which I saw but did not feel, then she wrapped the body of my child in paper towelling and gave it to the orderly.

'Take this to the incinerator.'

It wasn't much of a requiem. But at last, even if only briefly, something had happened which contradicted the clinical language of abortion. You can terminate a pregnancy all right, but how do you carry a 'pregnancy' to a furnace? Of all that had happened, this disposal of my child's body struck me as being terribly wrong. Exhausted by pain and repeated injections of pethidine, still I knew that incineration in a garbage disposal unit was not a fitting way to treat even the remains of a 'product of conception'. There should have been some kind of marker, something more than to be tipped into a furnace with the trash. Then it occurred to me that it would be terrible if the child were to be thrown into the fire still alive. But I couldn't risk looking to make sure he wasn't. Realisation crept close, but somehow I was able to push it away.

Reality, for me, was a place where all that had happened was the end of a pregnancy. It had to be. Here there was no human being to have died, who required respect, a marker for his grave; no one who might suffer pain when he was thrown into the fire. I could not jeopardise that version, otherwise what had happened was straight out of Dante's *Inferno*. The orderly left with a small bundle wrapped in paper.

As I write now, years later, I wonder how my humanity could have been so mislaid that, at that moment, I did not feel the cruelty of what had taken place. How did I fail to see through the denial of the obvious, so extreme it is like voluntary schizophrenia, which must be achieved in order for such cruelty to wear the clothing of a simple medical procedure? I guess that only shock could so disrupt a normal human response, both to a child in the womb and to the destruction of that child. Certainly shock always accompanies death and, whether you think it is significant or not, a death *is* the outcome of an abortion.

Shortly after the orderly left, the nurse was called to the other woman's bed and the procedure was repeated. Another body was scooped up, wrapped and taken, I suppose, to the incinerator. Then the ward was quiet and I slept.

I woke at about six in the morning and I watched the light beyond the window panes breaking over the roof of the city, the towers and spires smoky-grey against the pale, yellow sunrise. There was no more pain, no more fear, only an emptiness which was almost peace. Light after darkness – it was over, or so I thought. Shortly after I woke I was taken down to the operating theatre where I was given a D & C, an operation under general anaesthetic in which the womb is scraped. This was to make sure that nothing had been left inside me, no part of the placenta that might set up an infection. I came round being sick, as I always am after a general anaesthetic. By late morning the effects had worn off and I sat in an armchair talking to the woman who had been in the bed opposite. Her name was Helen. She told me that she had had a cyst which had been growing faster than her baby and that she had agreed to an abortion because she had been told her life might be threatened otherwise.

By unspoken agreement neither of us spoke about the experience we had just been through, but there was an understanding between us – a mutual sympathy if not friendship. We would not meet again outside the hospital. Neither of us would want any reminders, that too was understood and accepted. Two other women were going through the admission procedure while we talked and one of them, now waiting for the medical examination before the abortion could begin, came over and chatted. She had short dark hair and spoke very fast. She was in her thirties and already had two children. She had a new boyfriend and this would be her fourth abortion. She seemed quite proud of the fact and talked about how fertile she was. I was shocked, but Helen went white. The woman moved back to her bed as the doctor came in but after the examination was over she carried on talking to us from the bed. Her first three abortions had been under general anaesthetic and each pregnancy had been by a different boyfriend. Helen rushed out of the ward and I followed her, seeing her distress. She stood in the corridor crying. When she could speak again it was as if she had become a different person. The gentleness, the quiet, considered tone of previous conversations had all gone.

'Make her shut up. She's a bitch. They ought to neuter her.'

I was stunned by her savagery yet at the same time I understood her feelings. The ward sister came up to us then and Helen exploded again.

'I never wanted an abortion. But that woman is boasting about it as if it was something to be proud of. You've got to shut her up. Give her some pethidine or something.'

'She'll not talk much any more,' the sister replied. 'They're connecting the drip just now. I don't think she'll be so quick to have another abortion after *this* experience. That's why we left her so long this time. It's no joking matter going through twelve hours of labour *and* an operation at the end of it. That'll make her think twice. Now you go and sit down and I'll get someone to bring you a cup of tea.'

The sister went into the ward ahead of us and I could hear her telling the dark-haired woman in the bed that she was causing distress and asking her please to keep quiet. I went back to bed myself and lay down. I did not speak to anyone else at any length again, but after a while I could hear another woman talking to Helen. She was the second admission to the 'abortion ward'. (I do not remember what the ward was actually called or how it was numbered, but they seemed to do nothing but abortions there and so it has remained for me the abortion ward.) I had only glimpsed her when she came into the ward – blonde, not very tall, a little on the heavy side, but then she would be. She had begun telling Helen her story. Just what we needed, I thought. Goodness knows how Helen will react.

As I listened, I realised that she wasn't a woman, she was just a girl. She was fifteen, she said, and she had wanted to keep her baby. She had not told her parents she was pregnant. She had not even been to a doctor until a week before. That was when her mother had found out. She was four months pregnant by then and she had thought it would be too late to have an abortion. She had been wrong. It wasn't too late. Her mother had arranged the abortion and had told her she would be thrown out of the house unless she did as she was told. So much for the right to choose for that girl, I thought.

Helen's reaction to the story couldn't have been more different from her earlier outburst. She was sympathetic and doing her best to convince the girl that the abortion was probably for the best anyway – to make the situation seem less bleak for her, I suppose. Well what else was going to get the girl through the next twelve hours? I don't remember exactly what Helen said. It was a good effort, but pretty meaningless. Nothing anyone said could have changed what was happening to the girl. We all had stories, but I thought they were probably best untold. I shut off, closed my ears. I was still exhausted and I went back to sleep for most of the day and the next night.

In the small hours of the morning there was a scream followed by a crash. I heard the nurse and an orderly, maybe more than one, come running in. The girl was crying hysterically and she had evidently pulled the drip out of her arm and knocked the stand over. I heard the nurse tell her not to look and then bark the order to the auxiliary to 'take it to the incinerator'. It seemed that our fifteen-year-old had sat up when she felt the baby being expelled from her body and looked at it. What she had seen had sent her into hysterics. I could well imagine why it might. It has been known for children only two weeks older than her own to survive – although it is a near miraculous occurrence. Her child would have been about nine inches long and perfectly formed, only needing time in order to be able to survive outside the womb.

The girl was getting more and more hysterical and I heard the nurse send someone to get a tranquilliser. Shortly afterwards the ward was quiet again. Then I put the pillow over my head and went straight back to sleep. There was a low moaning coming from the woman who had so upset Helen, but I really could not have been less interested.

The next morning I went home. Before I left, one of the doctors gave me a pep talk about using contraception, along with a prescription for the pill. I do not remember whether he was young or old, tall or short or fat or thin, but I remember that he made me feel as if I had been a naughty girl – not for having had a sexual relationship but for having committed the social misdemeanour of our age, that of having had an unplanned pregnancy. I had to promise not to be a bad girl any more, to use contraception in future so that I didn't cause any more problems for myself or other people by getting pregnant again.

He meant well, I know that, and in his way his intention was kind. But my problems were human problems of responsibility and maturity, of sound judgement and self-esteem. The only solution he envisaged was a medical one – surgery to eliminate the disaster of pregnancy and a pill to prevent it from recurring.

Literally by 'taking the medicine every day', I was to be innoculated against any further risk of disaster. My mind, my feelings, my soul, simply did not figure in the equation.

Perhaps that is because we live in an age which demands easy answers. The value of painful human effort to solve painful human problems is gradually being replaced by the quest for quick, technological solutions. But I have learned the hardest way possible that the 'easy way outs' of our time, the quick solutions which by-pass the need for effort, the need to suffer for what is right or worthwhile, which even by-pass our biological structures, these bring their own horrors with them.

For me, the affair with David, the child we had conceived so thoughtlessly and the responsibilities I had been faced with, had been my own, individual human disaster story. But I was not called upon to think through or to try to put right my mistakes. I dealt alone, if 'dealt' is the right word, with the emotional problems which had led me into the relationship with David, with the wounds it had left and with the emotions that finally sent me to the hospital for an abortion. These problems did not seem to concern those whose job was merely 'looking after a pregnancy'. (And therein lies the difference between a healer and a technician.) There was no message of hope, of acceptance without judgement; no suggestion that I might be a person fine enough and capable enough to be not 'a girl who had been caught out', but a mother who had been entrusted with the care of a new human being. Instead society, via its medical profession, simply offered an escape from disaster via an operating table and a contraceptive pill. I believe that I was worth more, human beings are worth more, than to be patted on the head like delinquent children and given a pill instead of the truth.

More than ten years later I still wonder, where were those who had the faith in God, in themselves and in others to look at the apparent tragedy of a nineteen-year-old pregnant girl and see in it the potential for great good and, eventually, great happiness? Where are they now? How many people would see abortion as the 'compassionate' solution and so perpetuate the belief that the beginning of a new life is a tragedy, that the pregnant mother is not a human being capable of extraordinary things and that there is no one who can bring good out of evil? And it is beginning to dawn upon me that ours may be the generation that has finally lost faith in itself and sight of what it means to be human.

I left the hospital that morning simply grateful that the nightmare was finally over. I felt free again and deeply relieved. True, my pregnancy *was* over, but something else was just beginning. So much of our experience of pleasure or pain is relative to greater joys or greater pains. What we think unbearable may only seem so because we do not know how much worse the alternative would be. The fear, distress and mental confusion caused by a pregnancy which is unwanted can seem so great that any escape route, however illicit or dangerous, seems preferable. I believe that is the trap into which falls the vast majority of women and girls who choose abortion.

If you know how to listen you may hear a terrible silence in the aftermath of their escape. In that silence is the unspoken agony of thousands who have discovered that abortion creates its very own, unique kind of torture which only begins after the fact – and for which there is no quick, medical solution.

Chapter Five

On the following Monday I was back at university. Since I was only in my first year, the pressure of work had not yet become intense and I caught up with my peers without much difficulty. Outwardly, there was little to show that I had been through anything more than a minor illness. Something within me, however, had changed fundamentally – only it expressed itself in ways no one else was permitted to see; in the very way in which I thought and felt and interpreted the world.

I was constantly afraid: afraid of rejection, afraid of failure, afraid of being alone. (Most people experience these fears from time to time. They aren't unusual, but neither are they healthy. They become abnormal and especially unhealthy if they dominate most of your waking life.) I felt like a victim, constantly under threat, but incapable of helping myself. I had no means of helping myself. In the first place, my feelings about myself were all destructive. I was afraid of rejection because, at some level, I really believed that I deserved to be rejected. And then, even if I had believed I was entitled to ask for comfort or help, I couldn't admit that I needed either. It was like being two people. One was ridden with anxiety, the other denied that the feeling even existed.

Oh, I felt the anxiety all right. I just didn't acknowledge the discomfort or the pain as being anything abnormal. As long as I didn't think about it I could ignore it and I didn't wonder what was wrong with me or why I was so afraid. I didn't want to know what was wrong, of course. I didn't want to think about the abortion, or about what I had done, or what had been done to me. And so the conscious part of me carried on as though everything were quite normal – never admitting that there was another, very different part of me which was afraid and in pain. There were signs of my real state of mind, of course, though I took no notice of them.

I still refused to decorate my room on campus. I still needed the anonymity. Having no wish to be reminded of myself in any way, I avoided leaving my own personal stamp on my surroundings with as much determination as my fellow students tattooed their imprints on theirs. Then there was my writing. Like so many other students I privately wrote poetry, about the thoughts, feelings and experiences that affected me deeply. I had written poetry since childhood – exuberant 'purple' verses that erred on the side of sentiment and cliché. Now, if I wrote anything at all, it was stark, bitter and satirical.

It had begun to matter more and more what other people thought of me – and less and less how well I did on my course. Because I was so afraid of rejection I became unable to take pleasure in the friendships I was offered. I could not believe that they would last. The time I spent with my friends, even those I had felt closest to, including Robbie, was no longer something to be enjoyed, but an exercise in proving to myself that I was still an accepted and acceptable human being.

Inevitably, I was in a continual state of tension.

Robbie and I were still seeing one another, but I was convinced that it could only be a matter of time before he found a way of ending the relationship. And then the girlfriend, who had hurt him so intensely by ditching him a few months earlier, began 'bumping into us' in the places we haunted, the places which we thought of, as students do, as being peculiarly 'ours.' Now that he was no longer pining for her, her interest was rekindled. Rather than have him drop me, I pushed him into phoning her and asking her out. After all, I reminded him, he and I were merely old friends who had been there for each other for a while. When he telephoned to say that he and Caroline were back together I said I was glad. And when I had replaced the telephone receiver I sat for hours in dry-eyed agony because he had abandoned me, as I had known he would. Years later he told me that he would never have left me if I hadn't virtually ordered him to, that with me he had begun to be happy for the first time in months. I had pushed him away because I couldn't believe that.

The truth was that I couldn't stand myself. And if I were detestable then how could I deserve to be loved by anyone else? My self-hatred made it desperately important to be accepted and liked by other people – and impossible to believe that I could be. Consciously or unconsciously, however, I avoided the possibility of any confrontation with my own emotions or anything resembling self-awareness. I worked hard at living only on the surface of my thoughts and feelings. I pursued a frenetic social life and was rarely, if ever, alone – constructing a lifestyle which let me live in a kind of blindness, let me avoid knowing what I really thought of myself, avoid knowing what I was doing to myself. I was, in fact, rejecting myself as absolutely as I had rejected my unborn child. And by refusing to allow myself to think, to consider my deeper emotions or my standing in my own eyes, I was passing sentence without any right of appeal. It was a strategy of self-annihilation. It is no surprise to me now to read the occasional newspaper account of a woman who has committed suicide and find, usually added as an afterthought, the information that she has undergone an abortion in the months before she killed herself. (For a fuller discussion of post-abortion trauma, see the Appendix at the end of this book.)

I remember the rest of that university term as a complete blank, a kind of non-living. The Easter holidays followed and afterwards came the summer term. I had gone home for the long weekend of half-term. My chaotic family was gathered together, high as overcharged batteries as usual, raging at each other one moment, helpless with laughter the next. Nothing ever seemed to be normal in our house. We just didn't seem to produce any of the quiet peaceable types who make life comfortable. As the weekend wore on I became aware for the first time that I did not feel part of that familiar, infuriating household. There were the usual intense discussions, the usual bickerings and the usual idiotic games, but they no longer seemed to have anything to do with me. I was on the outside with no excuse for being there. I wasn't pregnant any more. The whole episode was more or less forgotten about. But still I stood on the outside watching, unable to become involved. And that was how it began, as a realisation, finally, that something within me wasn't working properly.

I suppose that Christianity had always played a part in our lives. Through my childhood it was a truth guaranteed by my mother's say-so. Although I didn't wholly trust the convictions which were still, as far as I was concerned, a part of my childhood dependency on my mother, they remained more or less in tact. By that I mean that if questioned I would have said that yes I did believe Christianity was true. It just didn't seem to have very much to do with real life, or at least with my life. That weekend a friend of the family, who also happened to be a Catholic priest, was staying in the house. He had been given my bedroom and I had been put in what we euphemistically called 'the study'. (Actually, it was an all-purpose depository which might have been better described as a junk room!) Before supper our guest celebrated mass and I watched the breaking and sharing of bread around a table in our home.

I started hurting then without knowing why. It had something to do with my sense of alienation from the people I loved, but it was not only that – and it would not go away. Later, when supper was over and the household was going to bed, I picked at my feelings the way that children pick at a sore place. I pushed and probed, but all I discovered was that in the place where love and trust and joy ought to have been, there was only a kind of hardness. This discovery frightened me and now I became aware of the other emotion that I had been living with for weeks, never turning round to look at it or give it a name. At last I acknowledged my fear, and though I did not realise it that was how my healing began.

After the family had gone to bed I lay in the darkness of our junk room alone with the awareness of fear and pain, a pain like despair, that had settled in to chew through my insides. And then those emotions took on a distinct shape and dimension. Not only would God no longer love me, but he probably wouldn't even want to look at me after what I had done. It was as simple as that. I had had no doubt that having the abortion was wrong. Now the scale of that wrong measured itself for me in a banishment from all that was good and true and right. But I must have had some hope or some memory of that promise of forgiveness, which is the centre of the gospel of Christianity, because as I realised what I was most afraid of I called in voiceless desperation, 'Please, Jesus, help me.' I called and I was answered.

One moment I had been struggling with a pain greater than I could stand, the next it was as if the pain had moved to a great distance from me. Where I was now, was full of an immense, unquestioning love. It was not that the door had opened or a man had physically walked into the room but, just as certainly as if he had, I was no longer alone. There was nothing to be seen in the darkness and yet I knew exactly who was beside me. I do not know if there is any adequate way of describing his familiarity. I have never had a 'religious experience' of this kind before or since (at least nothing that was anything like so tangible). Nevertheless, I felt that I had known this person all my life and that he represented everything that was most precious to me.

What followed can hardly be called a conversation. It was an exchange made up partly of words, partly of images but mostly of something which I can only describe as understanding. I knew very well that what was happening was a miracle, but I was neither surprised nor overawed by it. It's a funny thing about miracles that when they are actually happening they seem to be the most natural things in the world. (Ask anyone who has experienced one!) They are so natural that everything else seems not-quite-right by comparison. There were no heavenly choirs, no trumpets, just the unannounced arrival, of the God I had called out to, and a change from one moment to the next just as if the July sun had come out on a February day. So I did not tremble in awe, or even question the miracle itself – only how and why it could possibly be happening to *me*. That seemed very surprising indeed. The man in the darkness seemed to smile and the smile contained a question: 'Why are you so surprised at that?'

'Because I did not think God could be there any more – not for me.'

The reply came as an image of a well with a low wall around it and a round, wooden lid stuck firmly on it, and I understood the image as if it had been explained to me. The water in the well was like my relationship with God and with everything that comes from God. (It occurred to me later that he likes the water metaphor. It turns up a lot in the gospels!) The lid was mine too. It represented my decision to close off what I saw as a dangerous hole that I might fall into!

Life with the notion of a God, an abstract God, whose nature and purposes can be played with as an intellectual pastime, is much more pleasant than life with a personal God who knows us intimately and who expects the same standards of behaviour that we, consciously or otherwise, expect of ourselves and others. It is much safer and more comfortable to pretend that if there is a God we really do not know what he is like; to pretend that the divinity is so far removed from us that our ideas of right and wrong are quite different from his (or hers). It is, of course, only pretence. For which of us *really* wants a God in whom there is, perhaps, compassion and pity and love, perhaps 'sublime radiance' (a phrase I read somewhere!), but not justice or honour or truth? It's just that we want the demands of God's justice and honour and truth to interfere with other people's lives with corrupt officialdom or merciless bureaucracies, but not with our pursuit of our own, personal desires. Most of all we are afraid of the demands which justice makes. We are afraid to apply its standards to ourselves. We are afraid of the implications of guilt and punishment and retribution.

And so I had sealed God out of my life. Now I understood – with that force of revelation which says, 'Of course, how could it have been any other way?' – that I had always known this God, this Christ. It was as if I had forgotten him and now, suddenly, remembered. But how could I have forgotten what, in that moment, was so clearly the most important thing in the world? This, it seemed, this was the source of my grief. I must have been very far away indeed to have forgotten him when I had needed him so badly. Never mind the fact that only minutes before I had thought of him only as an idea. Now I had no doubt that I would find him in my earliest memory, recognise him in my most secret longing and find him in all that I really loved. I had always needed him, had forgotten and betrayed him – while he had never forgotten me. And it seemed that while I had been far away from him I had been far from myself. Now he brought me back.

Something like ice had started melting inside me and all the trapped and frozen emotions of the past months were freed. I think I spent the rest of that night in tears that seemed to be the unshed tears of a lifetime. At least it seemed as if I wept for hours. In fact it may only have been minutes. Time didn't have very much meaning at that point. I wept for myself and for all the pain and fear and darkness I had created for myself. Then I wept for the child I had rejected. At last I could feel peace beginning – but there was still something that ate at me.

When you were very little, perhaps you did something which seemed to you to be so terribly wrong that you were sure your parents would never love you again if they found out. You were consumed by grief and fear because the loss of their love meant the end of all happiness, the end of all possibilities. And then your father picked you up and held you and promised you that it would be all right and that he would always love you. And the nightmare that had come true was just a bad dream after all. Perhaps looking back now you can see that the terrible and insuperable objects to the love and safety you wanted so much and thought you had lost for ever were, for your parents, quite easy to resolve. For your parents, your anguish was more important than any wrong you might have committed, however terrible. Well that was exactly what it was like. I was still 'in trouble' and I knew it. But someone who felt like a father and a brother and a friend had suddenly and silently taken charge and I knew that everything would be all right. Most of all, this someone loved me just the way that parents love their children, wanting not to punish but to comfort, not to condemn but to heal, not to judge but to guide.

'Show me what you have done,' says the father to the child who has been too full of fear, guilt and misery to dare to tell anyone what he has done. Then the child realises that his father already knows what he has done and still loves him anyway. The nightmare was, after all, a lie and the 'terrible thing' isn't going to happen. He may be in trouble, but the guilt of his secret crime no longer holds the power of terror over him. 'Show me what you have done,' said the God who was with me, and I began to explain, showing myself the truth as I did so. I was no longer afraid to look because Christ, who knew without asking, who knew better than I did what I had done and what I had become, had already looked – and still loved me.

This is what I saw. I may or may not have been ultimately responsible for the death of that child (though it is a responsibility which I accept without reservation), but one thing could not be denied. For the period of his whole life from the time of conception, my child had been dependent on one human being and one only. What he experienced of the light and sound and taste of the larger world, he experienced through me. Who else was there to love him, to be glad that he was alive, to be on his side? Growing inside me, I was his whole world and all that he had. And I had turned against him to the point of wishing, aiding and abetting his death. Only the worst kind of monster, surely, could be so pitiless? As soon as the thought had taken shape I recognised it, not only as the truth, but as the source of my deepest pain.

This, I am certain, is why so many women cannot grieve for a child destroyed by abortion, because grieving would mean facing this realisation. And who could live with horror on such a scale? In fact, although we may not acknowledge it or know it consciously, many aborted women do know this horror intimately. It is the unnamed fear which is the source of so many of the neuroses suffered by these women. It is the motive for many of the self-destructive acts and the phobias which have no obvious explanation. Because, however hard we might try, we cannot make the monstrosity of what we have done go away. We dare not look at it as a possibility in case it is true, so it lurks in the unconscious and we fight it hopelessly. We cut ourselves off from the 'dangerous' feelings which might lead us back to face it. Still we live with the secret suspicion that we are 'monsters' at heart, just as we live with the punishments we inflict on ourselves in a tight, vicious little circle of escapism and self-torment. It was against this knowledge that I had built my emotional fortress; against the remorse for having done this pitiless thing which could never be undone, that I had built a shell to block out every emotion which might have betrayed me to the truth.

Now, suddenly, I was seeing clearly again I was looking at what had happened and allowing myself to feel honestly – even though the pain was terrible. I was able to do this for one reason only. Someone standing close beside me already knew all this. He could see it all too – and far more – and yet not for an instant did he withdraw his complete and unconditional love. To him I could acknowledge that I had been the world to someone I had hated without reason – or thought I hated; that I had condemned to death someone who only had me to speak on his behalf. To him I could say that I was sorry, that I hadn't realised, that I would undo it if I could. And I knew that I did not stand condemned.

I was still weeping, not for myself any longer, but for the pain and the fear my child might have felt in his dying, for all the beauty of the world lost to him and for all the richness he might have brought to it. I knew now that I had never hated my child. I loved him and would have done from the beginning if I had allowed myself. Fear and my own cowardice had warped my perceptions of what was happening to me so that I had been unable to experience that love. And now it was too late. I could live with the fact of what I had done, but I did not think I could bear the emptiness of never being able to make it up to my little boy, never being able to tell him that I did love him, after all.

All of this, of course, I was sharing with my visitor. There was no option really because he was with me even within my own thoughts. He seemed to be prompting me to put into words what it was I wanted and so I did: 'Just to tell my child that I am sorry and to know that *he* forgives me.'

67

For the first and only time during that encounter my reply was given to me not in an answering love or a simple image or a flash of understanding but in words. Christ said: 'Don't you understand that what you did, you did to me? And I forgave you a long time ago.'

And with the words came the image of Calvary, a cross on a hill and a sky behind it that was red with sunset and black where the night was descending. How can I explain this or find words which are more than merely banal or overused? I had been forgiven two thousand years before I lived and that forgiveness had waited through all the intervening years for all that I would choose to do; for my rejection of a little helpless child and for my desire to be forgiven. Calvary was real. It was for *me*, personally, as it is for you who read this. And more, the miracle of Calvary had transferred the weight of that rejection to a different victim. I do not understand this and perhaps there is no human way to understand it. It was my child who died, but it was Christ who became the victim of my rejection and of the violence of that rejection. And one more thing became clear to me: in and through Christ my relationship with my child was no more dead than Christ himself. In loving one I loved the other. In being loved and forgiven by one I was, mysteriously, loved and forgiven by the other – and death truly has no dominion.

For a Christian there is this hope. There is nothing which God cannot heal. Abortion cannot be undone, but like any sin the world has ever known, it can be redeemed. The terrible rejection which it involves can be forgiven and undone. The death of the child remains a constant – but if God can suffer and forgive it then it only remains to desire and accept that forgiveness. It is as simple as that. When the crime

68

involved has been forgiven, all that remains of suffering is the death itself and the loss which death entails. Nothing in Christ, however, is really dead and nothing is lost.

This is not a theoretical idea. Death really *has* been destroyed. To be part of the body of Christ is to be part of all those who are alive in Christ whether on this earth and in this time or beyond what we call death — not symbolically, idealistically joined to them, but literally and really. Aren't you always a part of your family though you may not see them for years and years? If your parent or your child dies, do you not still feel the part of them that is within you, that is the love between you? Does love die? You have lost nothing through death except the joy of their companionship in this life. All that has happened is separation, the pain of parting.

How do I know this? I know it because what I had received was a complete healing of the breach of love I had committed. It was not a promise of healing in the future, a promise for something after death — but here and now the restoration of love and with it the restoration of my relationship with my child. Now I could mourn him. Now I could miss him. Now I could wait in hope for the time when we would be together again. There was nothing left to torture me. I was free to forgive myself and to love my child as God had intended.

Calvary had ceased to be history. It had become the act of love which released me from my self-loathing and gave me back what I felt I had forfeited every right to, my child and my life — my literal, real life here and now, not just my hope of life in the hereafter. The resurrection had ceased to be something you 'sort of believed in'. It was a dazzling miracle which had entered my own life and reunited me with the child I had rejected and lost. 'Someone saved my life tonight' go the words of a pop song. Well someone really did save my life that night. For me, Calvary happened in the darkest hours of the night, in our junk room at the front of the house. Someone gave his life for me and rescued me there and then. And that is really what Calvary means for each of us in the present moment, whatever that moment is. I finally fell asleep in the small hours of the morning, completely at peace, and the gratitude I felt then has never left me.

Perhaps you will understand why, for some time after that night, the sight of those who call themselves 'enlightened' Christians, particularly 'clerics' (for want of a better collective noun), mouthing their reasons for recommending abortion on 'compassionate grounds' enraged me – and worse. I had no right to such feelings and I try hard not to alllow them living space any longer. But still when I hear them, there are questions that burn me, so I will indulge a little and allow myself to ask them here:

What special knowledge leads them to believe that they have plumbed the mystery of creation and know its bounds, know when the sacredness of life begins?

What divine grace gives them the certainty, not only that God will understand if a woman has an abortion, but that *she*, the woman, will understand and be able to forgive herself?

What kind of blindness have they taken on, as if it were actually wisdom or insight, that they place themselves in the position of recommending a woman to go to hell? (I do not mean the hell that we are told waits for the wicked after death, I mean the hell that is living out a horror story in which you feature as the chief villain and your victim is someone that you never really stop loving.)

I know what it is to find that abortion offers the only apparent escape from an unbearable situation. I know what it is to choose that escape – and then to wake with an emptiness inside me as if some thief had come in the night and stolen a part of me. I have spent weeks and weeks after that, feeling as if part of me had died, feeling fear and anger and isolation without knowing why. I have lived at war with myself, repeating and repeating my own 'evasion tactics'.

Every aborted woman has evasion tactics. Usually these are the reasons why she *had* to have the abortion, the reasons why there was no other option possible. Often they include the argument that 'it wasn't a baby yet', or that the woman doesn't believe that it was a baby. The purpose of these tactics is, of course, to evade the possibility that you are responsible for the death of your own child, to evade the mind-numbing loss and the terrible, relentless remorse. My own tactics did not include 'justifying' the abortion or trying to convince myself that the child wasn't really human. They consisted mainly of telling myself that the child was dead anyway. I calculated over and over again the latest possible date of conception, the youngest possible age of the child at the time when the ultrasound scan had shown it to be thirteen weeks. Nowhere did I find the absolute proof I needed that I was not in any way responsible for the baby's death.

I have found myself, at last, with the nightmare staring me in the face, knowing that whatever you want to call it – foetus, product of conception or collection of cells – it was *my* baby that I had carried for four months, *my* baby that I had rejected to the point of wishing him dead, *my* baby whose death I had arranged. I have seen myself become, actually and irreversibly, the kind of person who would wish my own baby dead. There is no human action I could possibly take which would give me a chance *not* to be that sort of person, no way to undo what my baby had suffered or to make it up to a dead child.

Yet, as I was to learn, this horror can be faced and accepted and finally lose its power over a woman's mind and heart. I was to learn too, however incredible this sounds, that the child a mother has had aborted can become a source not of sorrow but of joy, not of guilt but of the certainty of God's love. It takes a kind of miracle, but miracles are far more common and more easily come by than we think. This is a miracle which is not only possible but available for anyone who asks for it. It is like a packet which has your name on it waiting for you to collect it. The only thing that was special about what happened to me was that my packet happened to be hand-delivered – and there was probably a very good reason for that! It is likely, I think, that the One who delivered it intended that I should let others know that their own gifts were waiting, uncollected. I am doing my best to pass on that message now.

We all seem to have a very hard time, however, believing in anything as simple as the miracle of God's love. We question it or flatly disbelieve it every day in hundreds of ways. The more complicated our lives, the more complicated we imagine the way to work them out must be. The worse the crime that we commit, the more difficult it must be to obtain forgiveness. Abortion is one of the most self-destructive acts a woman can commit, one of the most complex in emotional terms and one of the most serious crimes against an innocent human being. Even so, forgiveness, restoration, the healing of the mother-child relationship, these can be the gifts of a moment. All they require is the willingness to face the truth, the desire to be forgiven and trust in that forgiveness.

Of course, although this is simple, it is anything but easy. Moreover, it is not only the abortion which requires healing, but all the circumstances around it and behind it, the history which has led to it, the habits and attitudes which made it possible. Even the miracle I was given did not automatically transform my life. It was, rather, a starting point from which I have progressed on a sort of 'three steps forward, two steps back' basis to the present day. True, I resolved to be a changed person from then on – which probably lasted for about a week! This isn't nearly as strange as it sounds. To begin with, as I have already said, I wasn't what you would call a committed Christian by any means. Besides, change cannot be imposed like a set of new teeth. If it is to be a genuine change of heart and will, it has to come from within, with your co-operation and not like a piece of dental surgery.

And so my miraculous encounter did not undo all the habits of mind and action which I had acquired over the years. Instead, it became a kind of rock in my life; sometimes a foundation stone on which I could build my understanding and my faith both in God and in myself, but more often a sharp boulder on which I foundered when old habits or the persuasions of the world around me had taken me too far in the wrong direction. And in the same way that it worked into my whole life and is still working now, the miracle of that night worked in the long process of recovering from my abortion.

To speak of a long process may sound like a contradiction since I have already said that the elements of healing are simple. So they are, but that does not make healing either an easy or an overnight accomplishment. On the road to complete recovery there are very few short-cuts. It can happen that an aborted woman suddenly gains understanding and faith in the truth, although far more often this part of the process also takes time, but it is by no means the end of the story.

In saying that even a miracle is not the end of the healing process, I do not want to imply that what happened to me was only a minor incident or that it did not intervene in my life in a decisive and fateful way. The road to healing may be a long one, but the journey itself is barred to a woman who is imprisoned by her own guilt, who cannot bear to look at what has happened to her, who cannot grieve for her child or face herself. To be freed from that prison is not to make the transition to complete healing instantaneous, it is to make it possible.

Chapter Six

There was a heatwave that summer. It really began in late spring when spring and summer seemed to arrive together. Suddenly there were daffodils everywhere and all over the campus butter-coloured gorse released its sweet, apricot smell. The hills above the campus were covered in purple heather and the woods on the lower slopes, which reached right down to the halls of residence, were full of bluebells. If I had followed my own inclinatons it might have been a time for rambles and picnics in the woods, for Browning and Wordsworth. But that sort of thing wasn't very fashionable at the university, at least not with the image-conscious 'smart set' who mostly inhabited the night hours and coffee bars and pubs, and would have thought all that sort of thing very childish. Ours was the generation of Sylvia Plath and realism, of tortured self-analysis and the politics of revolution. We thought that we were enlightened. We had rejected the illusions of the innocent – in favour of the delusions of the cynic. How clever and how ugly was the world we had arranged for ourselves.

It wasn't easy, in that atmosphere, to begin the quest for a different reality – to find a single value that didn't just disappear when looked at from a different angle. And besides, I was looking for all sorts of contradictory things at the same time. I wanted to be accepted by those whose opinions mattered – the ones who knew that they were better than everyone else and who looked pityingly at the ones who didn't, at the awkward, the uncertain, the 'failures'. I wanted to prove that I was a success, one of those who mattered. And I wanted to be loved – not for its own sake, but to prove to myself that I was a worthwhile person.

With hindsight, I suppose most of us were looking for the same things and for very much the same reasons. The game was not to *appear* to need acceptance or approval from anyone else. I played it better than some, but worse, I think, than most because I was more desperate than most. As the immediacy of my mysterious experience faded into memory, it became increasingly urgent to find reassurance from those around me. I wanted proof in flesh and blood that I was the kind of person who deserved to be loved, accepted and approved of. And my wanting was conditioned by the fact that I was convinced of exactly the opposite. This, of course, is not a problem peculiar to the post-abortion psyche. I had been convinced of my own unworthiness to be loved and approved of for many years, since childhood. Later experience has taught me that this is true of most of the human race. But until I ceased to be absorbed in the secret of my own worthlessness, it never occurred to me that anyone else struggled to conceal the same dark spectre from the eyes of an unfriendly world.

Now that we have come to it, what do you really feel about yourself? Do you hope that other people will accept you, while secretly believing that if they knew what you were really like they would shy away in horror? Are you afraid of rejection because that is all you think you deserve? It is a very common blasphemy, and the cause of a huge amount of the pain we suffer. 'Blasphemy' is a strong word, but not too strong for this. If it is true that we were made in God's image, how can we be without value – unless God is without value? Isn't that blasphemy? If he, who had never known death or decay, loved us enough to take human flesh and to die for our sakes, doesn't his love make us worth loving – unless we say that God's love is worthless? And isn't that blasphemy? And yet so hard do we find it to love and value ourselves that many think love of self is a sin and some even consider self-hatred to be a kind of Christian virtue, instead of a profanity that contradicts the greatest truths of our faith.

Of course, what we usually mean when we speak about 'self-love' is really self-indulgence and self-interest to the detriment of others. That is not love at all, however. When you love someone you don't indulge their greed or meanness or selfishness. You want and expect what is best and most admirable from them and you do your best to help them achieve it. Above all you see the person you love as someone who is capable of what is best and most admirable. But that isn't usually how we see ourselves or even how we think we *should* see ourselves. And so it isn't coincidence that in every other context love means something fine and good, but applied to ourselves, self-love or love of self has come to mean something to be avoided and despised.

This affliction is almost part of the human condition. Even the healthiest of us has to deal with our own inability to love ourselves. It is when this inability to love becomes self-hatred that you really have problems. Abortion makes it much more likely that a woman will begin to hate herself and to act in self-destructive ways. Although she is convinced she does not deserve it, she desperately needs love, acceptance and reassurance from others. From them she will get an image of herself that contradicts the terrible image she has of herself. That of course is what I was looking for and one of the reasons why it was so important to me to fit in with what my friends considered the right attitudes and conventions.

I had, however, begun to want something else also, something more substantial. I wanted more of the mystery that had touched my life with the glimpse of a truth so powerful that it could turn time and space upside down, with the ease of a conjurer who knows how the ropes and pulleys work. Only I didn't want it enough to be prepared to change my lifestyle dramatically. It was just as important to me that I should be thought clever and sophisticated and be accepted as an important member of the crowd. (A vanity typical of teenagers, it is true. But how many of us really grow out of that one?) And so I found myself on very strange ground.

I had had what is usually described as a 'religious experience' which had put beyond doubt, for me, the fact of Jesus Christ, God and man, of his crucifixion and resurrection. The last thing I was prepared to do, however, was to become a campus-Christian. Part of the reason for this was an uncommendable reluctance to be seen as a member of the most unfashionable group in the university. But it wasn't only that. Quite apart from their low social standing in the eyes of their fellow students, their brand of Christianity seemed to have nothing in common with the shattering revelation I had received. And I had not the slightest desire to join that we're-all-right-Jack-(we're saved)-what-about-you? brigade. They were a clique like any other, as far as I could see. They were also exclusive like any other, and terribly smug. I didn't want to wear that badge or talk their 'in' jargon. I didn't feel like congratulating myself on being saved. And I couldn't feel smug about it. All of which seemed to be necessary to being a Christian on campus.

It's only now that I know what I most objected to. Not by any virtue or goodness of my own, in fact because of the very opposite, I had been placed at the cutting edge of

Christianity – at the place where the God of absolute goodness is no longer just an idea. In that place, my own undisguised infamy, instead of remaining comfortably, or rather uncomfortably, in the background, had stared me in the face. This is an essentially Christian experience – and it is anything but comfortable! But in that place too Jesus Christ, the Man-God, had bridged the gap between goodness and infamy; had turned the normal laws of human experience, of time and space, upside down to do so. This doesn't seem uncomfortable at all. In fact it is profoundly reassuring, until you think about it. Then it dawns upon you that behind the mere facts of this universe are laws you cannot understand and that behind the reality you think you know is an altogether different shape.

As wonderful as this is, it is also terrifying. So whatever else it is, Christianity is anything but a safe, cosy religion. Now I expected to find a Christianity which reflected that; a Christianity that challenged the usual perceptions of what is real and important – or, at the very least, a Christianity with a sense of the miraculous. Of course I found none of these. Instead I found something jaded by long familiarity, something which had forgotten or wriggled out of the dangerous and the uncomfortable truths, and replaced them with formulas. In other words, I found a human church and immediately rejected it because I didn't like it. It didn't look like my own experience of God. 'My' Christianity, I decided, was therefore more authentic. (And far, far less demanding of course!) And so I became my own authority on what was acceptable and what was not, which meant that I could do more or less as I pleased within the limits of my own, unreliable conscience. And, whatever I might do, I would consider myself a better Christian than the milk-and-water bunch who, in my opinion, made up the Christian Union. It never occurred to me that I was displaying an arrogance even more unpleasant than the self-congratulation which I so despised in them.

I felt that I had to make some change in my life, however, which would honour the gift I had been given and allow me to do something for God. The theologians might argue themselves sick about what a loving God thinks of abortion, or when the soul of a child is present or when an unborn child counts as one of our 'neighbours' whom we have been told to love as we love ourselves. I *knew* that to God abortion is a tragedy. To him these children are just as important as their self-appointed judges. I knew that what had happened to me and to my motherhood was also an immense sadness to him. And this truth at least I was prepared to defend publicly, and so I started the first anti-abortion group on that campus.

I think this was my first experience of the divine sense of humour. There was I trying my hardest to be thought sophisticated and socially adept. I had avoided at all costs the ridicule and the contempt which I would have had to endure by joining the Christian Union. Now I found myself championing a cause which was so unpopular that even the members of the Christian Union didn't want to know! I manned my lonely little stall (two tables and a pile of leaflets in one of the university corridors) faithfully once a week. I, who had been so concerned about my image and being accepted, was spat at, sworn at, shouted at and laughed at – and it did me the world of good. The funny thing was that my self-image didn't deteriorate at all – quite the reverse. Very soon I didn't care nearly so much what people thought of me for speaking out against abortion. (Moreover, my own group had twice the membership of the pro-abortion group by the end of that year.)

I continued to do this work for the next ten years and it taught me many things. One of the most important is that all truth is part of God's message to us. It is a single message, whole and complete – but we are not. We are broken and distracted and we can take hold of the truth only in pieces, one bit at a time. (Here I do mean truth rather than just fact. Truth is not an opinion, however powerful your opinion may be. Truth will convict you in the depths of your self. And it will always require something of you – usually something uncomfortable!) But begin with whatever truth, however small, has become a powerful reality to you, with whatever truth you have taken hold of – and allow it to take hold of you. If you acknowledge, honour and live by the small piece of truth that is real to you, then gradually much more of the whole message will become obvious. I can guarantee this from first-hand experience.

I had a very shaky relationship with my Creator – the sort where I had rewritten most of the rules myself and created, in my own mind, the sort of God who had my own priorities and, in fact, obeyed my laws rather than the other way around. Much later, when I began to understand that I had done this, I came to feel a mixture of shame and amusement at my own stupidity. More recently I began to realise that such stupidity is very common indeed. People 'remake' God all the time to make him fit with what they think he *should* be like or with what they would like him to be. One person's 'god' thinks that luxury is a good thing. Another's tells him that only the right politics make you a good Christian. One person's god expects him to turn up at church regularly, but doesn't much care what else he does. Another's god requires that he publicly chastise his brother or sister for the good of their souls, but never examine his own conscience. One person's god teaches him to hate those who belong to a different religion, even a different Christian denomination. Another's god tells him that the rules in the Bible aren't meant to be applied too strictly. One person's god says that he needn't believe that Jesus was really God, or that miracles ever really happened. Another person's god says that abortion can be an act of compassion and may even be the right thing in certain circumstances.

There are many, many more and they are all false gods, the creations of our own prejudice or convenience or pleasure. My own 'creation' decreed that things like 'spiritual consciousness', meditation and 'awareness' were much more important than things like being truthful and going to church. But whatever else I did to remodel God along more comfortable lines, I never attempted to deny or distort what had been guaranteed to me by God personally. Through the eyes of his love I had seen the humanity of my child, and through his mourning, the sorrow of that child's death. Through his gift – as if it were the gift of Calvary itself – I had seen the depth of my own betrayal of my child, which he had paid for with his own life. God could have said, 'It's OK. You went through a tough time. Forgive yourself. You didn't do anything that bad.' He didn't. There are pastors who tell women who have had abortions that this is what God *would* say to them. It isn't. Abortion isn't acceptable to God. This was a truth given me through a miracle and extremely important in my life. I stuck by it despite reinterpreting just about everything else concerning Christianity, and gradually, over the years, it started to pull the rest of my life into line. Piece by piece it was to change almost every idea I had about 'life, the universe and everything'! But at the beginning, when I began campaigning against abortion, I had no idea where it would lead me.

One of the first things it taught me was that God doesn't look at creation the same way we do. We do look at things very much from our own point of view and we tend to imagine that God does too. When I began to present the arguments against abortion to my fellow students, I did so from the limited understanding I had of the subject. It seemed obvious to me that a child at the age of sixteen weeks was perfectly and recognisably human. The six- or seven-week-old embryo didn't look human to me at all. I concluded that there was something different about it which made abortion at that stage less obnoxious to God as well as to me. That was until Katya began talking about her abortion.

During the previous term my Polish friend Katya, a slightly plump, very pretty and outgoing girl had had an abortion at six weeks into pregnancy. She lived on campus, and since I had moved back into the halls of residence, we had taken to dropping into one another's rooms for coffee and conversation. When I started campaigning against abortion a strange thing happened. Katya began talking about her abortion almost to the exclusion of everything else. I don't know how many times she told me why it had been necessary for her to have the abortion or how many times she asked me whether I really thought that it was all right to have an abortion at six weeks and only wrong at twelve weeks or later.

I had become a member of an anti-abortion group, and at that time their constitution concentrated on tightening the laws against abortion after twelve weeks. (This was extended at the instigation of a friend of mine a couple of years later.) Over and over again I explained to Katya that she should forget about the abortion – apparently without convincing her. It was quite a different thing from a later abortion. Her visits started to become so tedious that I took to avoiding her. What I failed to realise was that she was suffering dreadfully from post-abortion trauma. I had never heard of this, of course, and still imagined that my own experience had been unique. Moreover, I had formed an opinion about the humanity of the child before the magic age of twelve weeks which made it impossible for me to equate grief, loss, remorse and even death with the destruction of a child at that age. Katya had always been a little eccentric and now it just seemed she had gone over the edge – in fact I thought she was nearly bonkers.

Since then, of course, I have met many, many women devastated by the deaths of their six- or seven- or eight-week-old unborn children, but at the time Katya was a revelation to me. The more I thought about it and the more I saw of her (since it was impossible to avoid her completely), the more I was forced to admit that she was terribly troubled by her abortion. Nothing I said seemed to provide her with more than temporary comfort. Something within her contradicted everything I was saying to her, no matter how much she wanted to believe me or how much I wanted to reassure her. In the end I had to re-evaluate the humanity of her child. I had to admit that her suffering was familiar to me and that its source was the same as my own had been. Unlike me, however, she was on a kind of mental treadwheel – an endless cycle of rationalising and justifying to herself her decision to have the abortion. It was a treadwheel driven by the guilt and grief which she was feeling, but was unable to acknowledge.

There isn't a magical point at which humanity develops in the child along with fingernails or a central nervous system or eyelashes. Katya's experience had proved that to me for the first time. Now it seems obvious to me that either all women who go through post-abortion distress are crazy or else any abortion, no matter how early, is the killing not only of a child, but of a relationship – the violation of a part of the woman herself – and distress is the natural human reaction.

I can't say that I then devoted myself to helping Katya to face and deal with the truth that was haunting her so fiercely. It took a long time before I had read and experienced enough to know either that hers was a common pattern or that there wa a way in which I could have helped her. I was also more than a little preoccupied with my own needs and emotions at the time. I was busy looking for someone who would love me and give me a sense of worth, and the dangerous thing about looking for anything is that you often find it.

I met Johnny on a Thursday at the end of May. He was selling records at a stall on the bridge where I had my pro-life stand. He was a second-year Psychology student with a drug habit and a fiancée, (Madeleine), both of which I ignored. He seemed gentle and insecure (which made me feel needed) and very safe to be with. Right from the start his feelings for me were powerful and even compulsive. Within a week of our meeting he had left his fiancée, who was almost a childhood sweetheart, to be with me. As a result she suffered a breakdown, failed her final nursing exams and eventually left Glasgow altogether to try to pick up the pieces of her life somewhere else. She was a very fine person and deserved far better than such shabby treatment. Years later, when we all met, I realised that Johnny really had loved her in a way that was far more genuine than his addiction to me. When Johnny and Madeleine met again, and I met Madeleine for the first time, there was still an understanding between them, something gentle like an old friendship which made me feel like an intruder.

I should have known from the start what sort of feelings obliterate the memories of years of loyalty and love, drive you so that you destroy the happiness, even the lives, of others. They are the emotions of compulsion. Passion, after all, is closer to addiction than to love. I took no warning however from the way in which my relationship with Johnny began, nor from the suffering it occasioned. I should have done.

The rest of that term passed very happily, apart from the recurrence of severe abdominal pains which meant that I had to be admitted to hospital twice. One of the most common post-abortion complications is pelvic inflammation. It is extremely painful and what is worse, it might have left me, like many others, sterile for the rest of my life. I was given an intensive course of antibiotics. When I was readmitted with a recurrence of the infection, I was warned that it was possible that both my ovarian tubes may have been blocked by scar tissue from the infection.

Being faced with the possibility that I might never be able to have any more children made me aware of another of the driving forces in my search for a relationship – the desperate desire to have a child, to fill the gap left by the abortion. I was using contraception at the time, since I didn't plan to have another child until I had finished my degree. But I remember thinking that I would rather become pregnant in the middle of my degree than live with the possibility of being childless for the rest of my life. There was a terrible ache where my first child should have been and the thought of living with that permanently was like contemplating a lifetime's prison sentence. I am far from being alone in this, for this too is a common reaction to abortion.

We have found that among women who became pregnant again after legal termination, 43.2% did so *within one year of the termination*, a figure in keeping with the results of Clow and Crompton (British Medical Journal 1973,1,321) who found 58% of women pregnant within one year of hysterotomy. [Hysterotomy is a very early Caesarian section performed in order to kill, rather than to save, the unborn child.] Either our contraceptive advice is not being heeded or these women consciously or subconsciously desire pregnancy. The social grounds on which the request for termination had been mainly based often remained unchanged at the beginning of the subsequent pregnancy (my italics).[1]

One of the characteristics of the abortion debate is the lack of common sense which seems to be available to the 'experts'. The bafflement at the idea that women who have already had a termination should then desire pregnancy would be funny if it weren't so sad. It is also extraordinary that no one seems to have followed up such studies as this (now fourteen years old) even from an economic viewpoint. If a significant number of women are becoming pregnant within a year of an abortion, and if these women are doing so in the same undesirable circumstances which led them to seek an abortion in the first place, then neither they nor society have been spared anything by the availability of abortion.

The single-parent family, the burden on the State, the disadvantaged child (all arguments advanced for social abortion) which would have been the result of the birth of the first child, have only been postponed for a year. Added to the cost to the State of the child of the second pregnancy (I argue from the economist's point of view here, not from my own!) are the costs of the medical facilities for the termination of the first child, the cost of whatever physical and mental damage the abortion may have done to the mother and the extra cost of medical care for the second pregnancy.

A plethora of medical studies show that women who have had abortions are liable to have more problems in subsequent pregnancies than women who have not. (In other words, a woman who has had an abortion previously is likely to need considerably more care through her subsequent pregnancies than a woman who has not had an abortion.) Those abortions after which women go on to become pregnant and have another child in the same 'disastrous' circumstances, have ended the lives of unborn children but gained nothing for their mothers materially, financially, physically or emotionally. There would seem to be, then, a significant number of abortions carried out in this country which, by anyone's standards, are a self-defeating waste of medical facilities, money, lives, health and happiness.

Yet again, however, it seems that nobody wants to look at this anomaly, let alone to rectify it. Why? I suspect that it is because the logical way to avoid this problem would be to make the criteria for abortion stricter. It would mean admitting that the terrible conditions which compel women to seek abortion cannot be so terrible as to warrant abortion after all since these women become pregnant and have a subsequent child in the same conditions. Of course 'terrible' is only a relative idea. The conditions which seemed impossible before an abortion have simply become less terrible than the longing for the child you have aborted.

I was to prove the truth of this phenomenon myself – as well as seeing it proved by several of my friends. I was never passionately in love with Johnny and I think I always knew that. Certainly I always felt a little untruthful about saying I loved him and a little bit guilty for feeling untruthful. What I saw in him was stability. His own problems only made it unlikely that he would ever leave me – even if he did discover what a horrible person I really was! So instead of being a disadvantage, I saw his shortcomings as a plus. I had secured the devotion I craved and the necessary support in which to have the baby I wanted so much. Consciously I still planned to wait until I had finished my degree before having another child, but I was being motivated by a need, perhaps an instinct, far more powerful than common sense or even ambition.

By September Johnny and I were living together in a cottage only ten miles from the university. By December, before the end of the winter term, I was pregnant again, but not before I had endured one of the most dramatic of all the effects of post-abortion distress.

Chapter Seven

At the beginning of August Johnny and I moved into
a farm cottage at a place called Piper's Pool, about ten
miles from the university. There were open fields
around it and little woods, which turned crimson as the
rowan trees changed colour with the autumn. We could
buy free-range eggs from the nearby farm and we
picked field mushrooms, ceps and chantarelles from the
meadow that surrounded the house. When the university term started, Andrew, a friend and fellow student in
his final year, moved into the cottage with us and we
divided the rent between us. We bought an old Morris
Traveller – which we called Henry – to take us to and
from the university, and Andrew became the 'official'
driver since he was the only one who had a driving licence.
For a couple of months everything went beautifully. I was
doing well at my studies. Johnny and I were happy and,
although the cottage was no more than comfortable, the
beauty of the countryside around us more than made up
for the lack of luxuries. Then, at the beginning of
October, it all went dreadfully wrong.

It started with something which seemed quite insig-
nificant, a bad dream. I dreamed that I was lying asleep
when a murderer silently broke into the house. Armed

with a knife he crept to the bed where I slept. I dreamed that I woke in time to see the knife descending and to know that I could not escape. In the darkness I couldn't see the murderer's face. I really did wake up then, shaking and sweating. Johnny did his best to comfort me, but it was hours before I was able to fall asleep again. A few nights later the dream recurred and this time, when I woke, I was convinced that the dream was a premonition. I was being warned of a terrible danger. I saw the dream not just as a symbolic warning, but as a literal description of what was about to happen to me. No one else in the house was harmed by the nightmare figure and so no one else had anything to worry about. It was only my destruction, while I slept in the darkness, helpless in what should have been the safety of my home, that was imminent.

From then on, night after night and sometimes during the day as well, I would be struck with terror at what I thought was going to happen to me. No matter where I was or what I was doing I was incapacitated by the onset of these attacks of panic. I began a ritual each evening. Johnny had to check every door and window in the house to make sure that it was properly locked, every cupboard and possible hiding place to make sure that no one had come in unseen, to wait hidden until I was asleep. But even this was not sufficient.

Once, sure that the murderer was outside in the moonlight, I climbed out of bed and pushed a solid mahogany dresser, that stood almost to my chin, across the room to block the bedroom door. The next day Johnny, Andrew and I had to use considerable effort to push it back again. Andrew climbed through the bedroom window to help us because Johnny and I couldn't move the thing by ourselves. Such is the strength that terror gives you.

On another occasion I hid a knife under my pillow at night and then buried it the next day – after I had convinced myself that the murderer would use it to kill me. To help reassure me, Johnny borrowed an old, lead-filled police truncheon from my grandfather (an ex-policeman) and slept with it under his own pillow. This made me feel a little better, but still time passed as if I were under sentence of execution. It was difficult to concentrate on anything. I couldn't sleep properly and exhaustion made it steadily more difficult to cope. I began to have panic attacks during the day when terror of what I believed was going to happen would seize me and I would become inarticulate with fear. 'Panic attack' is the only phrase I know to describe the phenomenon, but it isn't really adequate. The fear creeps up on you almost from nowhere and suddenly you are in the middle of it – a fear so strong it's paralysing. It makes your arms and legs hurt. When it is at its worst, you want to be sick and you can't stand up let alone walk. It even has its own smell.

Before long, my family and friends were becoming extremely anxious. It seemed inevitable that I would have to be taken into hospital for psychiatric care. It was Andrew who finally made me see that my behaviour was not exactly normal. He suggested that my nightmare had been Freudian – the product of my guilt about living with a man I wasn't married to. I was pretty sure that this was not the case because I had already lived with David and anyway, like most of my contemporaries, I thought very little about having sex with a boyfriend. It was the done thing and it certainly would not have caused me a crisis of conscience at that time. Discussing it with Andrew, however, made me realise that there was something wrong with me. There was not really some threat of destruction hanging over my head – however powerfully I felt it. I could see, though only just, that the real problem was the fact that I believed in this threat and was treating it as if it were real.

Once I had realised this, I was determined to fight my nightmares and to win. I started taking afternoon naps to catch up on the sleep I had been losing. I stopped taking the contraceptive pill in case it was causing hormone disruption. And when the panic attacks began I dealt with them by telling myself that the fear I was experiencing was itself the problem and that I would find myself still alive and in one piece the next morning. Gradually the fear began to lose its hold over me and I became more rational. It was only then that I guessed the real cause of my distress. It was associated with guilt all right, but not guilt over my sexual morals. This was guilt about the death of my child.

The image of a child sleeping, enclosed in the safety and darkness of the womb, is not so very far from the image of the person asleep and helpless in her home. The faceless murderer bringing sudden death was my own vision of abortion – from the child's point of view. At some level I knew in my own mind that I deserved to suffer what I had made my own child suffer. This had become a conviction that I *would* suffer in a way that closely paralleled the destruction of that child.

The human instinct for justice demands an eye for an eye and a tooth for a tooth. This is a very hard doctrine to dispel. Christ, however, brought a new and very different kind of justice. Because of his sacrifice, the demand of the old law for its 'pound of flesh' has been replaced by the possibility of forgiveness and healing. And because God has utterly transformed the kind of justice that we can expect from him, so we are expected to love our enemies and do good to those who hate us. But how hard it is for us to leave behind our human instincts for vengeance and the fear of vengeance. I am certain that these were the instincts with which I was struggling and which had trapped me into a waking nightmare. In a sense, it was a struggle between the old law of vengeance and the new law of God's love. For me, it was now a personal struggle. I could believe in my dreams of fear or I could believe in the truth of my encounter with Jesus Christ. They could not both be true.

I had already started to talk myself through the panic attacks. Now I would recall the memory of Christ's forgiveness and remind myself of the fact that if a death required another death to pay for it, then the payment had been made at Calvary. Christ had shown me that himself; that this payment had been made for me personally, as it was for each of us. I had only to remember and believe in him. Before long I was free of the nightmare and it has never recurred.

I have met two other women who suffered an almost identical problem, and I met both within two years of my own experience. Both had had abortions and both were undergoing psychiatric care. Neither, however, had associated the cause of their 'paranoia' with abortion — nor had the doctors who were treating them. One of my saddest memories is that of Jane, the first of the two.

She was about seventeen, an elf with dark hair that curled around a tiny face. I met her on a holiday, while I was spending a weekend with relatives. When I arrived, my aunt took me aside and explained that Jane was suffering from a mental disorder which caused terrible attacks of anxiety. That weekend, she had been allowed out of hospital to stay with my relatives, who were friends of hers. This had only been allowed because among the household was an experienced doctor, a consultant at the local hospital who would know what to do if there was an emergency. During those days Jane would be trying to do without the drugs which had been prescribed for her. The drugs suppressed her attacks, but they had fierce side-effects and Jane hated having to take them. They caused terrible physical reactions, resembling something like a fit. Her own doctor did not think she was ready to stop taking them, but since my relatives were willing to cooperate and since there would be a qualified doctor in the house where she would be staying, he had agreed to let her try. But this meant that she was bound to suffer from the anxiety attacks. In fact she suffered several of them over those few days.

I expected to be as helpless as everyone else when one of these attacks overtook her. To my astonishment I not only recognised the emotions she was experiencing, but I knew immediately and instinctively when they were about to engulf her. On the very first occasion, when the room was full of noise and talk and people, I remember that I saw a particular expression on her face and I asked her, quietly, if she would like to go somewhere else. We left the room together and I sat with her for the next hour or so. I didn't know then that she had had an abortion. All I knew was that she was terrified, certain of imminent death, certain that she had to die and equally certain that if she did not, then someone she loved would die as a kind of punishment. And I knew, out of my own memory, how to speak to her and how to help. I talked Jane through her terror in the same way as I had talked myself through it. I don't suppose there is a formula for saying the right thing. I think it was just that I recognised what she was feeling so completely that I knew, from one moment to the next, what would lead her out of the labyrinth of fear she was in. It's a bit like having mapped your way out of a dungeon. You know which doors lead where, which ones lead to more terror and which to hope and calm and reason.

By the end of the weekend she was beginning to confront her panic and to fight it. And she was beginning to cling to me as if I were a life raft. Unfortunately, it was time for Jane to go back to hospital and for me to return home. She didn't want to go and I would have liked to stay and help her. But I had already been asked not to interfere as she was receiving specialist help and a well-intentioned amateur could make things far, far worse. That was perfectly true and it would have been unreasonable to argue. Only my instincts told me that I knew the inside and the layout of the dungeon where Jane was trapped and that her psychiatrist did not. And I felt as though I were abandoning her.

About a year afterwards I heard more of Jane's story. She had been pushed into having an abortion by her parents less than eighteen months before I had met her. After that weekend with my relatives she remained in hospital for nearly two months. Then, only a few months after being discharged, she became pregnant again. She had the baby, a little girl, and kept her. It still hurts when I think about Jane, but I take comfort from the fact that she did leave hospital and did pick up the pieces of her life. And I hope, wherever she is now, that she is happy.

The second time I met this phenomenon was in a woman who had had an abortion fifteen years previously. She had been in and out of psychiatric wards for all those years, was undergoing psychiatric care when I met her and still is as far as I know. Nothing I could do or say helped her. Anna is one of the reasons I never forget to be grateful for the miracle that helped to heal me. When I think about Anna I know that that could easily have been me, and the thought of spending years and years living in that nightmare is sickening. Fortunately, this kind of crippling paranoia is not one of the more common reactions to abortion.

I am quite certain now that had it not been for the fact that I had already had an experience of God's forgiveness and of the restoration of my relationship with my child, I would not have recovered from that period in my own life anything like so easily. As it was things were pretty well back to normal by Christmas. And I was pregnant.

I didn't find out, of course, until the beginning of February. It wasn't the late period that alerted me. It was the onset of the same ghastly nausea, accompanied by a craving for red meat, which I had first experienced while living at Craignish with David. This time I knew what it meant. It wasn't until I was twelve weeks into pregnancy that I went to the university doctor, a Dr Cole, to have the pregnancy confirmed.

I guessed that he was in his early fifties, a small, bespectacled man with a kind face. I liked him on sight.

'Well, young lady, what can I do for you?' he asked.

'I think I'm about twelve weeks pregnant,' I said. His face fell.

'Oh. And what do you want to do about it?'

'Have a baby,' I replied. His expression changed instantly and he beamed at me.

'This will be the first confinement I have attended for years.' Then he corrected himself: 'Well, not the confinement itself, of course, but the first mother and baby I'll have looked after right up to birth – the first in a very long time. Right, let's see how far this pregnancy has got, shall we?'

He examined me and informed me with obvious satisfaction that I was quite right. I was twelve or thirteen weeks pregnant. We were friends from that moment on. Occasionally, when I went for my check-ups, we would discuss abortion and his position at the university. Dr Cole hated referring the students for abortion. He regarded it as a sad necessity, and anyway he didn't feel he had much choice about it. I don't think he had realised just how much he did hate it until I presented him with the job of helping to see a pregnancy through to term. He was peculiarly grateful to me for having the baby instead of an abortion; for involving him in the miracle of birth instead of the cycle of death. His gratitude was completely undeserved, of course, which made me feel a little awkward. And that was how I came to realise that abortion can hurt the people who are involved in the process of carrying it out, as well as the women who undergo it and the children it destroys.

One of the things I never confessed to Dr Cole was the fact that, despite my determination to do the right thing this time, and even despite my previous fear of never having another child after the abortion, I did not have the slightest maternal feeling towards this new baby. It was as if the abortion of my first child had cauterised the feelings which I should have had, and wanted to have, for the unborn child I now carried. Perhaps, unknowingly, I had abolished those emotions in order to go through with the abortion in the first place. I can't be sure of this, of course, but it does seem very likely. After all, how could anyone get through the medical destruction of their unborn child if she were already experiencing the emotional ties of motherhood?

Unfortunately, if I had banished those emotions previously, they now stayed banished. So, pregnant for the second time, I remained in a kind of objective separation from my child. What worried me most was that sometimes I really resented the 'little parasite' who was taking over my whole body and redirecting my life to accommodate its needs, whatever the cost to me. I did not want to feel this way. I wanted to be a good and loving mother. But the right feelings simply wouldn't appear to order. There was nothing I could do about that, so instead I set about behaving in exactly the way that I thought the perfect mother should behave – no matter how I really felt. It probably wasn't very good psychology, but I reasoned that if I behaved in a certain way then eventually the feelings might follow the pattern of my behaviour.

I prayed about it too, wondering if this was a kind of punishment for my lack of love for the first baby. I thought that maybe I was being shown that I couldn't pick and choose which of my children to love. Perhaps I was, but we do not learn this kind of truth as a punishment. I am sure now that it *was* a consequence of having rejected my first child, but a natural consequence – not a divinely imposed one. I had put an unconscious barrier between myself and my involvement with my first child, and I simply didn't know how to remove that barrier now that I wanted to. I think this is one of the examples of the way in which we hurt ourselves through sin – through actions which are not in keeping with the way in which we have been designed. In any case, I continued in this emotional state, distanced and slightly hostile towards the baby, until I was about fifteen weeks pregnant. Then, it seems, my prayer was answered.

One mid-April evening, Johnny and I had been to see a show at the university theatre. On the way home we took a short-cut to the bus-stop. This route cut across the back of the university. It was very poorly lit, in some places not at all. It was familiar to us, however, and neither of us anticipated any problem finding our way in the dark. What we had forgotten was that a large ditch had been dug recently – for a new pipeline to the science building. This ditch was some six feet deep and four or five feet wide. In the darkness I mistook it for the road and simply stepped out into it. I knew, as I fell forward into empty space, where I was and what must have happened. And in the same instant I knew how I really felt about the unborn child in my womb. When I landed, painfully but harmlessly, on the muddy bottom of the ditch, my knees were under my chin, my arms wrapped tightly around my legs, my back was arched and my head was down. I had gone instinctively into a tight ball whose centre was the child. I wept and wept – all the way home in fact (which must have been embarrassing for Johnny). And all I could think about was that my precious, helpless baby might have died because of my stupidity. That of course was the end of my emotional separation from the child and of my resentment against my pregnancy.

From then on I was in the grip of powerful emotions,

the strongest of which was the fear that I might lose the baby. I tried hard not to give in to worry or anxiety because I knew that these negative feelings could help accelerate a miscarriage. There wasn't any reason to think I might miscarry, but I had now formed the idea that the abortion might have damaged me physically in such a way that I would not be able to carry another child to term. Incidentally, that is sometimes the consequence of abortion and I had read enough on the subject to know this, so it was not an entirely irrational fear. Once I had passed the twenty week stage I began to feel safer and more secure about the baby's survival.

Later that month, Johnny and I were married. It was not, of course, the kind of wedding I had imagined myself having. Everything was very rushed. I had to borrow a wedding dress from a friend. I shook with nerves all the way through the wedding ceremony. And Johnny's mother didn't improve the reception by bursting into tears and telling anyone who asked that I had trapped her son and ruined his life. (In the end, my new father-in-law, usually a very mild mannered man, marched her out and warned her that he would send her home if she didn't stop it.) We spent a weekend at a Bed and Breakfast in the Lake District as a honeymoon.

Getting married was a mistake. It was part of my trying to do things the right way this time, but in fact it was only compounding the dishonesty of my relationship with Johnny. He and I were not just very different people. His habitual use of drugs whenever things became difficult meant that we had never faced our problems together. Drugs also helped him to shore up his image of me – which was what Johnny *really* loved – and to help him avoid accepting, let alone making a commitment, to the person I really was. For my part I had committed myself to a pretence and I knew it. The trouble was, I was pretending to myself as well as to everyone else and I didn't have enough courage to admit it. And so I woke up on the morning after my wedding knowing that I had done something disastrously stupid. Having done it, however, there was nothing for it, but to give the marriage the best effort I could and hope that somehow it would work out.

Driving to and from the university every day was more than I could take now that even the shortest car or bus journey made me sick. Johnny and I moved out of the cottage at the beginning of May and were given married students' quarters in the university for the remainder of that summer. We were told, however, that we could only live on campus until the autumn term started, when the baby would be almost due. The rules forbade students living in university accommodation with their children. We would not have chosen to stay there anyway. The 'married' rooms were cramped and things were already becoming difficult between us. Lack of space and the volatile state of my emotions accounted for many of the problems. The birth of the baby and somewhere reasonably sized to live in would make things easier, make it possible in fact to get down to sorting out our relationship – or so I hoped.

In the meantime I concentrated on my studies and the activities of the growing anti-abortion society which I had started at the university. I was doing well in my course and I was pleased with the numbers and the enthusiasm of the society. Then the group hit serious problems.

To be accurate, it hit one serious problem – the end-of-year student elections. Halfway through the summer term the election of officers to the Council of the Student Association took place. These officers would comprise the 'ruling body' of the CSA for the remainder of that term and most of the following year. Among other things, the CSA ratified grants to the various student groups, organised campus events and generally played a large part in student life. Most of their decisions had to be ratified in turn by a General Meeting of the student body.

The General Meeting itself had to be attended by at least ten per cent of the student body or else any votes taken were void. Neither condition was usually a problem for whichever political group had won the elections. Especially after the yearly elections, the meeting hall would be packed out by the supporters of whichever faction our fickle student body happened to be supporting at the time. Unfortunately for our anti-abortion group, this year it was the extreme left-wing group (an off-shoot of the Socialist Workers' Party), who swept all comers before it to assume control of the Student Council.

Immediately after the elections the Annual General Meeting of the Students' Union was scheduled. (This really just meant the annual meeting on behalf of all the students at the university, since membership of the union was compulsory). I didn't really pay a great deal of attention until the secretary of our anti-abortion group came to me with a copy of the motions to be proposed to the General Meeting. (Motions had to be circulated a week before the meeting so that counter-motions and amendments could be tabled.)

The document read like a 'purge' of all non-revolutionary groups and societies on the campus. It had been proposed that the Christian Union be disaffiliated from the Student Union and its funding removed. The grounds for this were that the Union was only open to Christians and therefore contravened the ruling which said that all student societies had to be open to any student who wanted to join. The hypocrisy of the proposal was stupefying. The Socialist Workers' Party was the first to throw out any member who didn't toe its political line down to the last full stop.

And immediately below this proposal was another motion – to disaffiliate and remove funding from the anti-abortion group – my group. The grounds given this time were the existing affiliation of the Student Union to the National Abortion Campaign and the student policy which supported 'a woman's right to choose'. In other words, our anti-abortion group was at odds with existing student policy. But then so were various other groups. Student policy changed from year to year according to the mood of the student body at that time. It was another piece of blatant skullduggery and I couldn't believe that it would be accepted. What was at stake, however, was not only our status as a student society, but the very right to organise meetings on campus, to give out literature or to do anything else which might dissuade female students from having their children aborted. No organisation was allowed to operate on the campus in any way unless it belonged to the Student Association or had the approval of the Student Council – and once we were disaffiliated we certainly wouldn't get approval from the Student Council. I had no alternative but to attend the meeting and try to make sure this didn't happen. I was almost six months pregnant, but we had no one else who could, or would, cope with public speaking.

I arrived at the meeting late – in time to hear the closing debate on the Christian Union. I couldn't believe what was happening. Speakers were refused permission to speak – on abstruse technicalities. The meeting was packed out with jubilant 'revolutionaries' (their term not mine) and the mood was unmistakable. They could do anything they wanted to and they would find justification in some regulation or policy – just by reinterpreting a rule or a policy statement to make it mean what they wanted it to. I watched in horror as, to the accompaniment of boos and jeers, the Christian Union was officially barred from membership of the Students' Association. Then it had come to the motion to bar our group. And I knew that my carefully planned speech was no use at all. This was a kangaroo court, its members turned out only to celebrate their new-found power. They would do whatever they wanted – and they wanted to silence those students who opposed 'the woman's right' to abortion.

I rose from my seat feeling sick. The lights were too bright, my hands were sticky and I thought that my voice might fail me. I wasn't a bad public speaker (nor a brilliant one either), but nothing in my experience had prepared me for this trial by fire. Speaking to small friendly groups was a far cry from speaking to a hostile audience of hundreds. I put my notes down on the seat and left them there, saying silently, 'Right, God, I can't do this. No one could. If you want me to continue doing the work I've started you'll have to take over. You'll have to tell me what to say.'

And I walked down to the podium without my notes and with no idea of what I would say when I got there. I remember the lights in my eyes and my own voice seeming to come from a long way off, but I don't remember what I said. I never was sure just what I *had* said. All I know is that the hall became quiet and when it was over my friends were on their feet clapping. Being obviously pregnant probably helped sway the decision, but I had no doubt what had really made the difference. That wasn't my speech at all. At the end of the meeting, when we had won the vote and everyone was leaving, various people came up to congratulate me. I didn't like accepting their praise, but I was afraid to tell them the truth; to say: 'It wasn't me, it was the Holy Spirit.' It would have been a very unfashionable even embarrassing thing to say, so I just kept quiet and felt awkward.

Once again I had seen how simple miracles really are. But most important of all I had seen that God had not only forgiven me, but that he was 'there for me'. He came with me right into the lions' den. And once again what struck me as miraculous was not the process of supernatural intervention. It had all seemed entirely natural. I had had no sensation of being 'taken over' while I spoke.

The thoughts had shaped themselves in my mind so that they had felt as though they were my own. Only there had been no effort on my part and I had not thought about the construction of the speech. It had seemed to construct itself. What really seemed extraordinary, however, was the fact that it had happened to *me*.

My encounter, some months before, with the forgiving Christ had released me from the tyranny of my own guilt and remorse, but I still had to contend with my sense of worthlessness – of being the sort of person who could act, indeed who had acted, out of fear, without love and against the very laws of human nature. I knew that divine intervention aside I deserved to be punished and to suffer. Having been forgiven for my crime did not make me, in my own eyes, a different person. Thus I was still grappling with my fear of rejection, with my complete lack of self-esteem. I no longer trusted myself, no longer believed myself capable of anything fine or worthy or good. God, it seemed, had had other ideas.

That meeting was another milestone in my life. God had taken control where I had been powerless and he had achieved what I could not. He could have let me suffer, but he didn't. He had allowed *me*, who surely least deserved it, not only the responsibility for defending the truth, but the role of his own mouthpiece. He had actually used me, had spoken through me, in the way that he had used the prophets and the apostles in the Bible. The idea was staggering. It is difficult enough to believe in God's unconditional forgiveness. It is even more difficult to realise that he means it when he says that there is no further penalty. He had forgiven me, paid the price for my failure and now, apparently and without any reason that I could see, he trusted me. It seemed that my inadequate belief in God was not after all the essential factor in my relationship with him. He had accepted my act of faith as he accepts even the smallest act of love or faith.

His response had been his act of belief in me.

Now I really understood what his forgiveness meant. First, there was no one left to whom I had to say sorry, no one left to whom I owed a debt of guilt, no one left with the right to judge or condemn me. Then, he had become the common bond between me and the child I had sentenced to death – and in such a bond there is only love. Thus he had restored the proper relationship between me and my dead child. Now he had shown me something of the person he believed me to be – the person he had created me to be. I was someone he trusted, even with something as important as his own message. It was a very different picture from my own image of myself.

No one sees you the way you really are except God, and no one except God knows the 'you' that you were really meant to be. What is so difficult for us even to imagine, let alone believe, is the generosity of that vision. It is important to try to believe in it, however. It is important to know that God sees you as someone more wonderful than you can imagine. Despite the fact that we all constantly fall short of his vision of us, that vision remains constant and gives us all an ideal to be faithful to. Simply, if he believes in us then we can believe in ourselves. He has given us each a self that we can love and be true to – and return to when we have fallen short of what he knows we really are.

Since that first glimpse of God's faith in me, I have been trying, clumsily, slowly and usually unsuccessfully, to let myself become the person he showed me then – to let him make me that person. I have also tried, ever since then, to convey the same unconditional approval, the same belief in a wonderful potential to other women tortured by the abortion of their children and the horror of what they fear they have become in the process. That is the hardest thing of all to do. It is hard enough in the face of a woman's own hatred and contempt for herself. It is especially hard in the face of those who feel that women who have had an abortion should be punished.

Unfortunately, there really are those who do not accept that it is right or proper – or possible – for a woman to be whole and happy again after an abortion. They are not evil people. They are no more evil than those who try to convince a woman that her abortion wasn't really a terrible thing and that God doesn't mind. Both attitudes are reverse sides of the same coin.

The first denies God's ability to forgive and heal completely. In effect it says that there are some crimes which are beyond even the power of Calvary and the Resurrection to restore. There are some acts of destruction so total that healing and restoration are impossible in this life. Not so. Calvary is a miracle so huge, that to wonder whether it can encompass either the greatest or the smallest of sins is sheer nonsense. It is simply bigger than anything we do or conceive of. Such vastness baffles reason and imagination. Nevertheless, if we believe in Calvary at all, then we must believe in it in all its impossible immensity and terror and awe. There is nothing that the death of God himself cannot put right, nothing which it cannot cancel out – this death which is so much greater than all other deaths, this murder so much worse than all other murders, this love so much greater than all other loves.

On the other side of the coin are those Christians who deny that abortion is evil, who do not believe that it really requires forgiveness and healing. These are often the same people who do not believe in sin at all. God, they say, is a loving God and so he doesn't see abortion as a great sin. (Actually, it is quite difficult to discover anything which they think God *would* regard as a great sin.) They fail to see that the more God forgives, the more loving he is. It is the reality of sin that measures God's love for us. These deniers also diminish, for themselves and others, the immensity and the mystery of Calvary. Since they refuse to accept that there is anything so very bad for Calvary to redeem, they make the death of God a useless sacrifice. If there is nothing really to be forgiven and healed and restored, at least nothing that merits the price God paid, then what was Calvary for? And if there is nothing really huge to be forgiven and healed, there is no huge act of love in God's unconditional forgiveness and healing.

Christian truth is almost always paradoxical. From one point of view the unbelievers and the deniers are both right. There is a deep betrayal implicit in the deliberate abortion of a child, a betrayal so profoundly inhuman that it demands vengeance. And, vengeance set aside, what human power can replace a dead child or forgive a mother on behalf of her child or reforge the bond between them? So, from a human perspective, abortion is unforgivable and irredeemable and, from a human perspective, the unbelievers are correct. From God's point of view, however, forgiveness is the act of a moment and Calvary has already encompassed and restored every act of destruction and betrayal ever committed. Then, in the light of God's death, we do not bear the penalty of our crimes and so in this sense, from God's perspective, the deniers are right when they say that there is no penalty for abortion.

One side sees only the human perspective, the other only the divine. But the miracle of healing can only be understood and, indeed, is only possible so long as you recognise both.

Chapter Eight

In August, Johnny and I found rooms about three miles from the university and moved into them. I began taking lessons in breathing and relaxation technique from the National Childbirth Trust. We painted the bedroom and filled it with things, ready for the baby's arrival. And then we waited – and waited! Our son was born on a grey afternoon in late September. I had planned a natural birth, but when he was three weeks overdue I agreed to have the birth artificially induced. The placenta was calcifying – hardening – and it would have been risky to wait any longer. All the same I used the techniques I had been taught by the National Childbirth Trust, avoided any drugs and was able to have the same midwife with me throughout labour as I had been seeing for most of my ante-natal care.

Actually I had caused the hospital a lot of trouble over this arrangement. At first, to Dr Cole's alarm, I had insisted on having the baby at home. I had notified all the relevant authorities of my decision and had been asked to visit the hospital to discuss the matter. Johnny and I made an appointment to see the relevant officer when I was about seven months pregnant. She was pleasant, friendly but adamant that I could not have my baby at home. There would be too much risk involved. She warned me that if I went ahead and had a home delivery the hospital would not undertake to provide me with medical care at all. I had checked my legal position carefully, however, and knew that the hospital was obliged to provide medical assistance. My interviewer was trying to frighten me into having a hospital birth. That was understandable. She was acting in what she saw as my own welfare and the baby's. In the event of an emergency a hospital is quite the safest place to be. But I had my own reasons for wanting to have my baby at home. I said simply, 'I think you should know that I have informed all the necessary authorities in writing of my intention to have the baby at home. If anything does go wrong during the birth you will be held legally responsible.'

The woman did not argue. She just sighed. I was quite right. She changed her approach.

'Look, why are you so dead against a hospital birth?'

I told her. I wanted a natural birth – no unnecessary interference. I did not want to be treated like a patient. Patients are ill and a healthy pregnant woman is not; pregnancy isn't a disease, quite the reverse. I wanted the baby to be born gently, not hauled out into bright lights and noise. (Contrary to popular belief newborn children are extremely sensitive to light and noise.) I did not want to be in the hands of complete strangers during the delivery, who might insist on procedures I did not want. I did not want to risk having one midwife with me for most of the labour and then have her change shift so that someone totally new, who did not know about the kind of birth I wanted, would appear to deliver the baby. And I wanted to be at home with Johnny and the baby afterwards, not in a hospital ward which Johnny would have to leave to go home by himself.

I was being bolshy and I knew it. But it was desperately important to me do the very best I could for this child right from the start. Everything I had learned about foetal development since I had begun campaigning against abortion more than a year before, told me that the newborn child is a sensitive, conscious being who is likely to be extremely traumatised by the experience of birth. I had been impressed by the work of Frederick Leboyer, a French doctor, who showed that a gentle birth made an enormous difference to a baby's comfort and security. I wanted that for my child.

And there was one other thing, one other reason why I did not want to bear my child in a hospital bed. Eighteen months before I had given birth in a hospital bed to a child too young to live. That labour had been a ritual of death. My child's body had been placed, not in my arms, but in an incinerator. I did not want to be reminded, while I gave birth to my second child, of the death of my first. If I were in hospital, however, I was sure that my surroundings would remind me constantly of the other birth, the abortion.

In the end the administrator offered me a compromise. The hospital would provide continuous care – one midwife who would see me for most of my antenatal care and would deliver the baby when he or she was born. The midwife, Johnny and I would work out a method of delivery together that was both practical and which would go as far as possible towards providing the kind of birth I wanted. I could leave the hospital an hour after the delivery as long as everything had gone smoothly. The offer was too good to refuse. I could have the best of both worlds, a natural gentle birth for my baby with the maximum possible safety guaranteed. It would have been purely selfish to turn it down. So I agreed. Unknown to me I had just become the subject of an extremely controversial experiment!

My pregnancy was monitored, not only from a medical point of view, but to see what sort of impact it would make on the hospital if other parents-to-be demanded the same sort of treatment. As it turned out things could not have gone better –even despite the induced birth. My labour was ferocious, but the techniques I had learned from the National Childbirth Trust meant that it took only four hours instead of the usual eight to ten hours of labour. Moreover, I had expected the kind of agony I had suffered during the induced abortion of my first child, but this was nothing like so painful. I needed no expensive drugs. I was not exhausted by the end of the labour and so did not need any help to deliver the baby. (The mother's exhaustion is quite a common reason for a forceps or caesarean delivery.) Isobel, my midwife, delivered the baby in a semi-dark room with great skill, and placed him on my stomach with the announcement, 'He's a boy!'

I was stunned – shocked might be a better word. He was so completely distinct and individual, a different person from me altogether, even a different gender. And I had no idea who he was. I knew that he had been used to hearing my voice while he was in the womb so I spoke to him quietly, cupping my hands around him as we waited for the umbilical cord that still connected him to his life-support system, the placenta, to stop pulsating. (It was important not to cut the cord right away because the baby can get oxygen from the placenta while his lungs adjust to breathing cold air properly.) All I could think of to say to him at first was a very wobbly, 'Hello, Matthew.'

It was followed by a lot of rubbish of the sort that people say to babies. Then Isobel cut the cord and lifted him, wrapped in the sheet that had covered us both, into my arms. He had stopped crying and was lying quietly, his skin against mine. Then he looked up. His forehead wrinkled as if he were concentrating hard, and his eyes held mine for a long moment as though he were making his own introduction. Then his eyes slid away, his gaze wandering around the room, exploring it. (Babies can't focus properly at first, but they can see.) After that, he was far too interested in what was going on around him to want to eat. He's been the same ever since, and as a result, mealtimes have always been something of a problem!

Johnny, Isobel, our student midwife Karen and I were all as elated as if we had drunk a bottle of champagne, and as triumphant as if we had scaled Mount Everest together. Isobel strode out and collared the consultant obstetrician. He had predicted that I would beg to be wheeled to the maternity ward after the baby was delivered. I would be exhausted and would want nothing more than to sleep for twelve hours, he had said. Isobel dragged him in to see us. I was drinking tea with one arm and cradling Matt, who was still lying back and looking around him, with the other. We all grinned at the consultant and he just shook his head and laughed.

'I told you so!' said Isobel – who was senior enough to get away with talking to a consultant like that.

'All right, you win. Well done,' he said and left.

'This,' said Karen, 'is how it should be. Birth should always be like this.'

She was perfectly right. She was thinking, of course, of the rather impersonal mechanised deliveries which, until Matthew's birth were all she had seen in that hospital. But I was thinking of another sort; an act of rejection instead of welcome, a birth that no one would celebrate, with no waiting crib and no future full of endless possibilities, just a paper towel for a shroud and an incinerator for a grave. That is abortion, the travesty of birth, some demonic caricature of what it is meant to be. Now I knew why I had been so determined to get Matthew's birth as right as it could possibly be. I wanted to answer the travesty of the first birth with something as close as possible to what God really intended it to be. I wanted nothing in the birth of my second son which in any way, even slightly, denied his humanity, his rights as an individual, sentient person. And that was how it had happened; the way, as Karen said, that it should always happen.

Matthew and I live together now, in the upper half of a Victorian house with a large garden for him to play in and countryside around us. He is a normal eleven-year-old, apart from the older-than-his-years wisdom that he has acquired from living with only one parent. His father left when he was two, which hit him hard even at that age. It was a bitter parting and I was left to bring up alone the child of a man I disliked. Moreover, it has never been easy to do so, either financially or emotionally. The irony is that I was left with precisely the same situation as I would have been had I kept my first child, David's son. And not for one moment have I regretted having Matthew, or blamed him for his father. In fact through Matthew, Johnny and I have learned a kind of respect for each other. Little though this is, it is at least honest.

I finished my degree before John left and, perhaps because it was important to me to prove that you can have a child and be successful, I took a good honours pass. But I did not begin trying to earn a living until he was nine. I was not prepared to leave Matthew in order to go out to work. It seemed hard enough that he should lose one parent. I would not deprive him of both. I remained involved with the anti-abortion movement, however. I wrote and researched and debated and met others who had been hurt by abortion. Eventually I began to recognise the pattern of post-abortion trauma in myself. I also found that I understood and recognised the pain of other women whose children had been aborted. It came as quite a surprise to realise how common and how typical the pattern of my own unhappiness and self-hatred had been. I had been too close to it before to see it. Gradually, as I retraced my own experience, I also realised how fortunate I was. And I began to try to understand the dynamics involved in post-abortion healing, as I had experienced them myself.

I began writing and speaking, in a small way, about the problem of post-abortion trauma and how to address it. I also began, again in a small way, working with women who had had abortions. You might describe what I did as counselling, but I prefer to think of it as befriending. In the process, two things happened to me which in a way marked the end of my own journey of healing.

The first was that I returned to the hospital building where my first child had died, as part of a peaceful demonstration. I felt a little strange about going back there, but glad too in a way. I thought it would be like a pilgrimage. As we approached the building, however, I began to feel more and more unwell. It seemed to be increasingly difficult to breathe. Then I blacked out. I don't faint. It just isn't something that happens to me. This was the nearest I ever came to it. It was like hyper-ventilating, when you stand up too quickly, except that it didn't stop. I wasn't aware of walking and I couldn't see anything except a spinning darkness, but I didn't fall over. Luckily, I was with an old and close friend who frog-marched me a little way from the rest of the group and sat me down on a wall.

Actually, hyper-ventilating was exactly what I was doing. My emotions were so strong that the effort to control them was making it difficult to breathe. As I looked back at the building, a drab yellow facade that stared back blankly, I felt as if I were looking at Auschwitz. I wanted to destroy it and scatter every brick. The rage and hate and grief were like physical entities. Trying to suppress them made me dizzy again. I had to get away from the place. My friend guided me away from the hospital, into a nearby park. As we got there I could hear someone screaming. It was an ugly noise, almost feral – like an animal bellowing. It took a few seconds to dawn on me that it was I who was making that horrible sound. The emotions I had ignored or expressed only in silence and in secret had found their voice. At that moment I had not the slightest control over them.

The park was empty and my friend was a dear one or the incident would have been far more embarrassing. I am not much given to 'primal' experiences, nor do I care for the sensation of being out of control, so this was a very distressing event in every way. But I think that it must have been necessary all the same. When I was calm again, much later, I decided that I did not want to destroy the hospital building. I wanted to empty it and turn it into a memorial to all the rejected, unborn children who had died within its walls. Perhaps one day all abortion clinics and wards will be recognised as the tombs they really are.

The awfulness of that visit made me feel very close to the child I had aborted. It made me wonder about some kind of memorial rite and what sort of marker could be made for a child whose grave was a hospital. I suppose that was what triggered the second incident.

I don't remember exactly what I was thinking about at the moment when it happened, only that it was about something fairly mundane. It began with the feeling that there was someone else in the room with me. Then came a mental image of a dark-haired, rather solemn little boy of about ten. He was mine; I knew that at once. Only I had always thought of my own child as a baby. This was a boy and – I worked it out – about the age he would have been had he lived. And he could see me just as I could see him.

It was an encounter which I cannot explain or prove was anything more than my own imagination. The mind is extremely powerful. On balance, I think I accept that it was what it seemed to be, not just imagination, nor a 'ghost', but a vision – only a two-way vision. (At the time I had no doubt at all that it was real.) He had the same distinctness, the same individuality which had overwhelmed me when Matthew was born. He had long limbs with light brown, out-of-door knees and elbows, and dark brown hair and eyes. They were David's hair and eyes, the features I had first liked about him. Strangely, I didn't mind that at all. It was just part of the miraculous way that children borrow their features from their parents and make them into something completely their own. There was also something about this child which reminded me of myself more than Matthew ever has. It was something about his expression and about the way, I sensed, he thought about things. That was a bit like cold water in the face. This child and I might have understood each other well. Only a parent could understand how precious such an understanding is. I had lost that possibility and it hurt.

But most of all he *was*. And I felt the same kind of pride in him, though tempered by pain, which I felt in Matthew. I knew suddenly that when people die they don't become, as I had imagined, half real, shadowy beings that are no longer recognisable. They remain themselves – and go on becoming more themselves. Whatever they were created to be, they shall be. Heaven is not less than the things we love, but more so, more truly them.

It struck me then that if this child still was, still is, then he was still my son and a member of my family. I had never given him a name, however, never acknowledged him as Matthew's brother. There was a kind of exchange going on between us, which I will not even attempt to describe, and it had led to this, that I should acknowledge and name him so that he would be more than a memory or a secret. I called him Thomas, Tom, in fact. He didn't 'leave' suddenly, the sense of his presence just became weaker until I couldn't feel it any more and I knew he was gone.

Whatever the source of this 'visitation', whether it was actual or created by my own mind, it taught me one last and very important lesson about post-abortion healing. The children who die are real and they never stop being so. The bond between parent and child not only can, but must be healed in order for a woman to recover completely from the abortion. Once that is accomplished, the dead child should, if possible, be named because naming a child is an acknowledgement of this bond. Not all women have a sense of the sex of their dead child, but a great many do and this obviously makes naming the child easier.

Those whom we love before death we go on loving after death. Their lives are honoured when we speak of them and remember them. Loving a child who has been aborted begins only after death, but the 'rules' are the same. They belong in our lives, and the memory of them belongs in our hearts, just as the name and the memory of all those we have lost go on belonging in our lives and in our hearts. Tom was and is my son. That meant that he was and is also Matthew's brother, part of our family. I knew that it was important to acknowledge him, his brief life, his continued part in my life, his relationship to me and to Matthew. I realised that Matthew ought to know about Tom. But how do you tell a child that you have had an abortion? I had always thought that I should spare him that.

At last, after careful thought, I explained to Matthew about his brother. He asked me some painful and difficult questions, but I had expected that he would and I answered him as honestly as I could. At last he said, 'You mean I've always *had* a brother." (Matthew has always wanted a brother.)

'Yes. I'm sorry.'

'Will I get him back in heaven?'

'Of course.'

He accepted the fact of Tom with a mixture of sadness and pleasure at the idea that he does, in fact, have a brother. And then, in the manner of most children, he got on with living. Matthew is no more preoccupied with the great imponderables of life than most children, but he has, on the whole, a pretty healthy understanding of his faith. And he does still mention Tom from time to time. Recently he announced: 'Do you know what I'm looking forward to most when I get to heaven?'

'No, Matthew,' I replied, distracted by whatever I was doing and not really listening.

'Meeting my brother at last. Seeing Tom, that's what.'

There really wasn't anything to say to that. It summed up so much of what we have both lost in Tom and of what we have been given back in hope; so much of what this book has been about. It would be far better if the terrible destruction of abortion didn't happen in the first place. After it has happened, however, there is a way out of the nightmare. There is a way not only to accept yourself again, but to live with the hope of being able to love and hold and be with the children we have lost. Matthew is looking forward to it. So am I.

Chapter Nine

Post-abortion distress – how inevitable is it?

It would make life much simpler and more comfortable if the effects of abortion were only theoretical. If abortion were, as it is presented, a crime against some religious idea, a crime whose effects – if they exist at all – are only visible on some heavenly scoreboard. It would be so much easier and more convenient if it were true that an unborn child weren't human, at least not human in the same way that the rest of us are human. The problem with this way of thinking is that it ignores simple common sense. There are things which will always be true and unavoidable about the effects of abortion, in just the same way as there are things which will always be true about our experience of fire, water, the pull of gravity or the changing of the seasons. Things as simple as instinct, logic and memory make it inevitable that a woman will experience some degree of post-abortion distress.

I do not say this only from my own conviction that destroying a child must have repercussions. Or, in other words, I do not say, 'It does because it *ought* to have.' The inevitability of post-abortion trauma does not depend on my own or anyone else's viewpoint. No matter what status you give the child in the womb – pre-human, sort of human or fully human – the basic laws of human experience dictate that some degree of internal conflict will afflict the woman who has had her child aborted. Often this will be a very great degree indeed. It may disrupt her whole life and it may occur years after the actual event.

I have said that there are consequences which are, and can be shown to be, unavoidable about abortion no matter what your viewpoint. There is a rider to this however. It is true that the inevitability of post-abortion trauma can be demonstrated from things which are a matter of straightforward, empirical fact. It is also true that the inevitability of post-abortion trauma can and should be demonstrated from the premise that human beings are created by God.

Human beings characteristically walk on two legs, have two arms, two eyes, a nose and a mouth. They do not have tails, are not covered in fur and they are mammals – they do not lay eggs. These characteristics are part of the description of a species. A creature with three arms, one eye and a tail would not strike us as human, or else he would strike us as a human being who had something terribly wrong with him. There are more subtle characteristics which are particularly human too. A human being will talk, sing, smile, laugh, reason, remember, love, play games, design, make and use artefacts. While we cannot be certain that no other species can do any of these things (whales and dolphins for instance may do a number of them), no other species does *all* these things. Moreover, the idea that an animal species can talk, sing, reason or smile does not suggest to us that we are like a particular animal. It suggests that the animal may be more like *us*, more 'human' than we had realised. To illustrate the point still further, we might say that a man covered in fur would remind us of a monkey, whereas a monkey doing a puzzle would remind us of a man. What all of this tells us, very simply, is that the human being is designed in a specific way. There are physiological and behavioural characteristics which are specifically human and others which are not.

However, the human being is not only designed to be a physiological and social being, he is also designed to be a spiritual being. What we know of that spiritual design is, first, that it resembles God's own nature. God created man and woman in his own image. Furthermore, we know that there is a difference between good and evil and that God is good. Thus we know that we were intended to choose good. When God had created man and woman he saw that what he had created was *very good*. In other words, it is not only in our spiritual design that this goodness is contained. But the design of our whole nature, physical and emotional and rational, in fact everything which makes us human is good in itself. We know also that because we have free will, we can choose evil instead of good. This means that we can ignore the way in which we have been designed and act in ways which are contrary to the nature which God created for us.

By a process of logic, we can say that those things in a human being which are not in keeping with the way we have been designed are not good. We would not call good an inability to walk, see, think, communicate, remember, love, or be happy. And we can choose things which actually damage our physical design – drugs and alcohol for instance. We can also choose to act without thinking, we can choose anger instead of joy, we can choose not to love. We know that choosing these things harms us and we usually judge them as evil.

We make value judgements all the time about our actions and the actions of others. These judgements come not only from a socially accepted moral code. They also come from our inner sense of the way in which we were designed. St Augustine says that we were born with the

121

memory of God so that we cannot help looking for him. We can only try to ignore that memory and the longing it creates within us. You could also say that we are born to be like God. We cannot help the sense of who and what we should really be. We can only try to ignore it. When we do ignore it, of course, we damage ourselves and others and we become less human in the process.

That is why, at some level of our awareness, is the idea that to be human means that we ought to behave in one particular way and not in another (for example, to show respect, compassion and fairness in our dealings with others). If this were not so, then why would we speak of some actions as being 'inhuman' and others as 'humane'? Interestingly, we reserve the label 'inhuman' for the very worst crimes we can imagine. In other words, within our very language we hold fast to the notion that the worst atrocities we can commit do not only injure their victims; they violate our humanity itself, they place us in some category other than human. It is also clear that we consider other kinds of actions to be proper for human beings and these are recognised as 'humane' or simply just 'human'. How often do we praise someone in authority or in a position of privilege by saying that 'so-and-so is really very human' or describe some act of thoughtfulness or compassion as 'a very human thing to do'? We already have the concept, therefore, of human and inhuman behaviour, a concept which is directly related to the idea of good and evil.

Knowing which is which, however, is not always straightforward. There may be times when it is not wrong to be angry, not wrong to hit someone, not wrong to take certain drugs. There are times when we have to make decisions about the rights and wrongs of a certain action. The wrong decision may be reached for the best possible reasons – but the reasons for taking an action can never alter its consequences. And, however hard we try, we cannot change the effect of an action by changing our opinion about it. Whatever is bad for us remains bad for us for as long as we remain human beings. Although we can justify almost anything we choose to do, what is evil does not become good because we choose to think it so, just as poison remains lethal even if we label it 'lemonade'. We have no control over the way in which we are designed. We cannot create ourselves any more than we can create daffodils or birds or stars.

The design of motherhood

Part of the human design includes, of course, what we call motherhood. Looked at objectively, motherhood is an extraordinary phenomenon. The fact that it is a characteristic which we share with many species of the animal kingdom doesn't diminish it in the least. Rather it suggests that it is a successful, powerful and, in some way, an especially important characteristic not only in our own lives, but in the creation around us. Or, in simple terms, I think we can assume that God likes this particular design feature!

Putting another person first, acting completely unselfishly, is not the easiest thing for any of us to achieve. Yet the onset of motherhood means that suddenly a woman regards the wellbeing of a person she does not know, has never even met, as synonymous with her own. The heroism of women when their children's lives or happiness are at stake is almost a cliché. Can there be anyone who has not read of at least one pregnant woman going through with a pregnancy which will certainly kill her in order to give her unborn child a chance to live? Motherhood, then, has its own, specific design. It may be extraordinary and illogical but only the very foolish would deny that it exists. It is unselfish, it is fiercely protective and it is intimately connected with the life of the child. It is much less connected with the experience of pregnancy itself.

123

Pregnancy, the early physical events in the lives of a woman and her developing child, is only a part of motherhood. Motherhood is a much bigger event altogether. It begins with pregnancy, but does not end when pregnancy ends. You can terminate a pregnancy, but not motherhood. Unfortunately, while it is difficult *not* to recognise and to react to the fact of pregnancy, under pressure you *can* fail to recognise or to respond to the part of you that has become a mother. For this reason it often happens that the emotions of pregnancy are quite different from those of motherhood. In fact, particularly in the first trimester, pregnancy is often so physically and emotionally uncomfortable that maternal feelings may be the last thing a woman is aware of.

It has been said that ambivalence about pregnancy is almost one of the symptoms of pregnancy itself – but no one suggests that a difficult pregnancy is the same thing as a difficult motherhood! In practise, however, that is exactly how a problem pregnancy is interpreted by our society in general and our medical profession in particular.

With an unplanned, problematic pregnancy a woman experiences (added to discomfort and hormonal disruption) distress, panic, even something like despair. (All the same, pregnant women are the least likely of any social group to commit suicide.) Her immediate feelings towards the child might be far from ambivalent. They might be downright hostile. Fear distorts. It produces anger, even hatred, for whoever or whatever seems to threaten you – even an unborn child. Fear, after all, isn't rational any more than love is. That does not mean that a woman will always feel the same way or that destroying the foetus in the womb is a loving and compassionate way to help her.

Think of a mother suffering from post-natal depression. The analogy is a close one. In this case too a woman suffers from a mixture of internal, hormonal and external problems. Treatment usually involves trying to alleviate the problems and generally do all that is possible to restore her to a loving relationship with her child. This is not done simply for the good of the child, but because it is the best and healthiest state for the mother.

For the pregnant mother, however, the treatment is different. She also has a child with whom she does not feel she can cope, to whom she cannot relate or else rejects. This fact, however, is ignored or denied. Instead, her desire to end the pregnancy is treated as a sound and reasoned request. The child is seen as the cause of her problem and so the extinction of the child is seen as the solution. It is as reasonable and as helpful as offering to smother the child of a mother suffering from post-natal depression. It is also very bad medicine. Abortion may end the immediate problems of an unwanted pregnancy, but it replaces them with others. When it is over the woman is left alone with the fact that she is the mother of a dead child. She is alone with all the emotional and psychological damage done when she becomes a willing party to the killing of her own offspring.

Pro-abortionists usually explain negative reactions after abortion in two ways. One is the supposed tragedy of destroying a 'potential life' and the other is the legacy of guilt left to society by the Christian religion. In fact, however, both are easily disproved.

The vast majority of women in this country do not disapprove of the contraceptive pill, nor even perceive it in a negative way. Clearly, therefore, the denial of a potential life doesn't create the same problem as abortion. But the pill will not only prevent conception from taking place, it will also prevent any conception which does occur from implanting in the womb, so causing an early abortion which a woman never knows about — although she knows that it is bound to happen at some time while she is using the pill. Morally and logically, this is just as much abortion as the surgical procedure, so a woman whose guilt was created for her by religious doctrine against abortion ought to be just as ambivalent about – even traumatised – by taking the pill.

Why doesn't this happen? I believe that it is because taking something which may cause an early abortion at some time in the future, does not involve the deliberate decision to destroy a specific child. A woman doesn't know about the children she loses through these very early abortions – any more than she knows about the children she may have lost through very early miscarriages. But she knows about the child she has aborted. She takes a conscious decision to have it destroyed. It is that decision, taken in the light of her knowledge of the child's existence, which violates her own inbuilt design in a way that the pill, for all its destructiveness, does not.

The design of motherhood remains after an abortion – no matter what personal viewpoint we choose to take about it and how good the reasons for the abortion. It can invest a pregnant woman with an intense love for a child she has never seen. It creates a profound sense of loss and grief in women who have miscarried a child – again whom they have never seen. (In fact, those who have lost a child through miscarriage will often continue to feel their loss for years afterwards, even when their grieving is over.) And it will create vicious and relentless guilt in those who have had their children aborted. It is a design which transcends both reason and experience – but since when have we ever pretended that the power of motherhood *was* reasonable or easily explained? How can anyone believe that the design of motherhood will suddenly bend to our own convenience when we tell it to and 'back off' because we believe that 'it wasn't really a baby' that died?

Those who deny the existence of post-abortion trauma have lost sight of the basic human design (and, I am temp-

126

ted to add, of common sense too). To put it into perspective, they are talking about the mothers of dead children – and mothers are almost always profoundly traumatised by the death of their own children. But they are not the only ones who have lost sight of basic human truth.

There are those on both sides of the abortion debate who weigh the interests of the woman against the rights of her child. For them it is a clear conflict – pregnant woman in one corner versus unborn child in the other. I think that both sides have made a terrible mistake about the shape of this battle. It is not surprising that advocates of 'a woman's right to choose' should ignore the humanity of the child in the womb. But when anti-abortionists press the claims of the unborn infant *against* those of the mother, they fall straight into the trap of regarding abortion as something which can be in a woman's interests – even while it destroys her child. Looked at from a different viewpoint, from the perspective of human relationship, both sides are setting one member of a family against another.

Ultimately, both pro- and anti-abortionists have left us with an argument which sets the wishes of a host, the woman, against the rights of a biological passenger, the child. And on both sides there is a complete failure to see the unity that is the woman *and* child – for a pregnant woman is not just a 'host' body, the child she is carrying is not just a passenger. That is only a description of their biological roles throughout a pregnancy, not of the relationship between them. And here is the heart of the matter: from the moment a woman becomes pregnant, a fundamental human relationship is established – the relationship between mother and child. How can the interests of a mother be weighed against the interests of her child without damaging the interests of both? How is it possible to harm a mother without hurting her child or a child without hurting the mother?

When we use everyday language, the language which describes actual human experience (instead of the language of the biology lab or of the political soap-box), then we remember what it is we are really talking about. Then the truth is obvious to us, for we all know what the design of motherhood entails.

It is, of course, possible for a woman to ignore the nagging of violated maternal feelings—but only as long as she is able to ignore the abortion. The problem is that life is full of things which are likely to remind her. Her peace of mind will then depend on her certainty of the arguments with which she has justified the abortion or, in other words, the 'reality' she has constructed to enable her to accept it; arguments about necessity, about whether it was really killing, about the humanity of the foetus.

The inevitability of logic

Thus we come to logic. The most basic statement we can make about abortion is that it is a two-option-only scenario. Either the foetus, or child, in utero is not a human being or else it is. Two possibilities follow from this. The first would mean that an abortion destroys a potential – not an actual – human being, in which case, though sad, it ought not to carry with it all the grief and the sense of loss which the death of a real child would cause. The other possibility would mean that an abortion destroys a very real, if very small, human person whose relationship with his mother has already begun. Anyone who is living with the memory of an abortion has realised this much, whether consciously or not, and she must deal with these two possibilities.

The truth simply must be one of these options. No matter what interpretation someone places on abortion there is no way to avoid this logic. You may choose to believe one thing or you can choose to believe the other. But if you do choose to believe that your unborn child wasn't really a

128

baby yet, or 'properly human', you will always live under the shadow of the other option and all that it implies. An aborted woman can never entirely escape the possibility that she has conspired against her own child – because she will never be able to prove otherwise.

On the other hand, unfortunately, there is no shortage of evidence to suggest to her that she has, in fact, engineered the destruction of her child. From the purely biological standpoint, we know that, the characteristics and abilities which will mark this distinct individual are present, already determined, from conception. From a very early age, no one knows how early, the unborn human feels the sensations of pleasure and pain and even dreams within the womb – of who knows what? Some of the most compelling evidence, however, is the psychological effect of abortion on the aborted woman herself.

For her the two possibilities about abortion are more than a philosophical exercise. If she chooses to believe that her abortion has simply ended a potential life then it will be that belief which defends her from her own remorse and grief. But it is only a belief – a belief that is never a proven, absolute, scientific fact. And within belief there is always doubt. The scientific evidence and the evidence of her own emotions will continue, inevitably, to stack up against her. Every fact about the development of the child in utero, every argument about the continuum of human life, every photograph from within the womb will tip the scales in favour of the idea that she has had a child destroyed. As the scale tips further, so the shadow of the abortion may well grow larger and more terrible, rather than receding gracefully into the past.

This is why I think that for very many women the memory of a pregnancy which ended in abortion is like a time-bomb waiting to go off. Perhaps it never will go off (in other words, a woman might never come face to face with the nightmare of seeing herself as her child's killer), but she must live with that possibility lurking somewhere in the background. And human logic is remorseless; in the dark places of your mind it asks, 'If abortion *is* killing a child then what does that make *you*?'

Suppose a woman turns to face this possibility, what then? What is she left with and how will she live with the knowledge that she is responsible for the death of her own offspring? I do not believe that there is any emotion more terrible than remorse – and that is precisely what waits for any aborted woman who finally acknowledges the killing of her unborn baby. So mostly we try to ignore the other possibility, never give it house room, rationalise our way out of it. And we live under its shadow and the shadow of our own doppelganger, the person we don't want to be, the one who had her child put to death, the one who waits in the shadow of that other possibility.

Sometimes a woman *does* acknowledge the death of her baby as such and, understandably, has to find some way of living with herself at the same time. Then instead of denying that she has accomplished the death of her child, she will attempt the even more invidious task of justifying the killing. But while she tells herself that the abortion was a sad necessity and that she had no other option, the doppelganger, creeps to the very edge of the shadow and comes to stand almost in the light.

Now the direction of logic becomes excruciating because it is very much easier, logically speaking, to decide that a foetus isn't a human being yet (despite the evidence to the contrary), than to convince yourself that the killing of a baby isn't completely monstrous or, in other words, that it was justifiable in your particular circumstances. If a woman can't convince herself of this, however, then nothing more will stand between her and the realisation of a living nightmare. What else would you call the growing conviction first that your abortion didn't just destroy a 'blob of jelly' but a living child; then that, without fully realising what you were doing, you have encompassed the death of your own baby and finally that there isn't any reason powerful enough to justify your action in your own eyes?

Studies have shown that a number of women go ahead with an abortion already convinced that it is wrong and that they are ending a human life by so doing. These are the women who are 'against abortion in general', who see abortion as murder, but regard themselves as exceptions to the rule or regard their own decision as 'justifiable' killing. In many articles and interviews you will find such a woman explaining, not that abortion is really all right, but that in her particular circumstances it was the least bad of a set of very bad options. Let's consider that position, and its implications for the woman, very carefully.

The woman in this position has already invested abortion with a negative moral value. Already she does not see it as just a clinical procedure. To go through an abortion with this objection already conscious in your mind is to leave yourself with only the device of somehow justifying this act of destruction as your defence against the crime of infanticide. A woman tried for this crime in a court of law would stand a much better chance of receiving understanding, leniency and compassion from the court than she stands to receive it from herself. A court would not punish her so mercilessly, nor for the rest of her life.

Just as I began what I hoped was the final rewrite of this chapter, I came across a newspaper article written by a woman who had had an abortion five years previously. Perhaps nothing really happens by chance. At any rate I include an extract from the article which gives a personal account of much that I have been trying to describe here.

The writer had tried, before the abortion, 'to put all thoughts of the baby out of my head, to treat it as a mere, not quite human foetus'. She failed. So she tried to find a justification for what she herself describes as murder. She

131

apparently failed at that too. But the pregnancy was uncomfortable, she had a very demanding baby to deal with and she had an unsupportive husband whom she risked losing (implied) if she did have a baby which he did not want. She had to find a way of living with herself and with her decision, and so she did. Instead of attempting to deny her child's humanity or to find a good enough reason to have him or her killed, she made her decision according to her husband's wishes, not her own:

> I awoke feeling positively elated ... For two months I felt truly happy. I was amazed at my apparent power of recovery and bemused at my lack of guilt. I've since read that this feeling of elation is quite common ... I was not prepared for the plunge into deep, dark depression I experienced shortly after that. It was like falling off a cliff you didn't know was there.
>
> I was watching a television documentary one evening that involved scenes of a pregnancy and birth. Within seconds of them showing that tiny newborn bundle I was in floods of hot, bitter tears. My sorrow was immeasurable, penetrating every fibre of my being. I was wracked with sobs ... for an hour.
>
> After that day I spent three months plunged in... the depths of anguish, anger and despair. I cried day and night for my lost baby. I wanted my child desperately and could hardly come to terms with the fact that I had been directly responsible for my own child's death....
>
> One night, wracked with guilt and desperately, desperately sad, I got down on my knees and prayed. I cried out for forgiveness and help. Eventually I felt a calmness and began to become more like my own self. But even now if something emotive appears on TV or in the paper I get a lump in my throat and occasionally have a cry. I'm crying now as I write this. [N.B. Five years later, ed.]
>
> I don't know to this day whether I'm pro- or anti-abortion... Life is sacred but it is certainly not simple.[2]

Earlier in the article this woman tells us that she had

already decided, before the abortion, that it would be killing a tiny human being. In fact, she already thought of it as 'murder'. She didn't really want the abortion (how many women do?), but felt compelled by an unsupportive husband and her difficult situation. So she began the post-abortion phase at the point which so many women try to avoid reaching, where 'the other option' was a reality for her, where she had had her own child put to death.

What kind of person did she feel she was, and what did having the abortion do to her self-image? She had done something, she says, which she had been against all her life. In her own eyes she had failed herself and the child she was carrying. 'My subconscious mind told me I was wicked.' Despite this remark, guilt is not the thing which really carries across from this article. This is partly because she has prayed for, and believes that she has received, forgiveness. It is also partly because she does not take sole responsibility for her action. She blames her husband, and with some justification. The abortion was her husband's choice, not hers, and by allowing him to make the decision for her she has, in a sense, shifted much of the blame onto him. But at the same time she has become a victim herself.

She has become powerless — as powerless to help herself and to take control of her own life as she had felt she was powerless to save the child she is still mourning. Moreover, her husband's rejection of the child, his 'cold cruel' demand that she have an abortion, his failure to behave like a 'true', supportive partner, have created an animosity in her which is tangible. She paints him eloquently, as an inhuman tyrant — almost the same way in which many aborted women see themselves.

Hers was what David Reardon in his book *Aborted Women* describes as a 'decision to be weak'. For her, logic now dictates that she cannot take control of her life — because if she does, then she will also be acknowledging her own power to choose, her own responsibility. To believe that she can be strong would be to believe that she could have fought for and had raised, without her husband if necessary, the child she had aborted. And, logically, if she *could* have been strong, could have had the child, then she must be responsible for not doing it; she will be 'guilty' in her own eyes. This has become her 'other option' and it continues to haunt her.

It is not difficult to see how, simply out of the two-option-only scenario, profound post-abortion trauma can arise even in a woman who is not deeply troubled about her abortion to begin with. The logic is simple and quite ruthless. If you cannot convince yourself that an unborn child is not really human yet, then abortion is just infanticide by another name. If abortion *is* infanticide, then unless you have a very powerful defence, you are a murderess. If there isn't a good enough defence (and there usually isn't any that will satisfy your own, internal judge and jury), then you have to try to find some way of living with yourself. It may be by punishing yourself, or else by accepting the role of a victim yourself whose own helplessness absolves her from the responsibility of the abortion. In any case, whatever the method, it isn't usually very successful, and guilt, remorse and self-hatred are common, and often permanent, post-abortion reactions.

One of the prerequisites, not just to happiness, but to what we call normality, is the belief that you are basically an OK sort of person. It is the belief that you are worthwhile (Christians have this on God's say-so!) and therefore worthy of love, friendship, joy. These are things which we were meant for and which we need as much as we need food, water and air. If you are afraid, or secretly believe, that you are a monster, a mother who has killed her own child, then you will never quite believe that you are deserving of love, acceptance or happiness. You will not be able to give or receive fully.

You may even cut yourself off from these things as a kind of punishment or become afraid of losing them as 'punishment from God'. (A surprising number of non-believers have said that they were afraid that God would punish them.)

It is, of course, possible for a woman to construct a complete rationale for her abortion – and believe it. It *is* possible to ignore logic and the direction in which it is taking you, at least for most of the time. It *is* also possible to avoid exposure to facts about foetal development or photographs showing the child in utero for most of the time. Let's say that she doesn't have to consider whether or not her abortion killed a human child. She doesn't think about it. It's possible. Or it would be if we were not subject to the tyranny of our own memories.

Memory

One of the most important faculties we have – and also one of the most challenging – is memory. Whatever happens to us in our lives is 'internalised' through memory. That is to say, as soon as something happens to us we begin to deal with it, to evaluate it and decide what it means to us, by remembering and reliving the experience. Reliving memories in this way can help us to accept and come to terms with negative experiences. It can help us understand why we behave in certain ways, perhaps by unlocking some previously forgotten episode in our childhood. Sometimes we call on memories of happy occasions to cheer ourselves up or to boost a low self-image. And the reliving of memories is one of the most important ways in which we grieve for someone.

We release the person we have lost with every memory that comes back to say: 'No more. You shall never do this again or see this or laugh in this way again while you live.' We call on memories to help us make major decisions in our lives – like whether to get married or not! We can go back to something that happened in the past again and again through the years and we can gain more, or different, insights from the recollection as we come to understand more about life and about ourselves. The point is that memories are living things. Any event in our lives, any experience we have had, goes on affecting us through memory, conscious and unconscious, all through our lives. And we remember far, far more than we think we do.

What about the memories that are just too painful to deal with? What about the ones that make us feel frightened, insecure and, sometimes, worthless? I think, in fact, that we have all run from memories, pushed them away and tried to avoid their implications at some time in our lives. In some extreme cases people have spent their whole lifetime trying to escape from their memories. It has driven a few to despair or madness. They run because memories can recall things which have become too painful to think about or because sometimes memories might tell them things they do not want to know. Whether we like it or not, however, memories cannot be escaped. They do not go away, at least not permanently. If we ignore them or blot them out they still go on affecting us even while we deny them. We may still feel frightened, insecure or worthless because of past experiences, but we just don't remember where these feelings are coming from. We either try to pretend that whatever it was never happened or we pretend that it was perfectly all right, that our memories of it are fine. Doing this, memories become prisons unless they are finally dealt with, and such prisons have their own kinds of torture. It is a torture particularly well-known among aborted women.

No one on either side of the debate pretends that abortion is something a woman ever forgets. She will always live with the memories of that experience. Aborted women re-enter their experience with each article or TV discussion which they see on the subject and with each of the reminders that daily living is liable to throw up from time to time. Every time that she does remember her abortion, she must reinforce her justification for it. This isn't always easier with the passage of time. In fact a woman whose abortion is very recent is often much less troubled by her experience than one who has been living with the memory for years. Every reminder, every 'flashback', can trigger a variety of emotions, guilt, anxiety, sadness. Eventually, they may simply trigger a treadmill on which a woman repeats the pattern of memory, re-examination and reassertion of the justifications for her abortion. Or they may initiate a depression that becomes part of the cycle of her life. It all depends on the extent to which a woman has dealt with what has really happened to her.

Usually, however, an aborted mother cannot begin to face what has actually taken place. She cannot acknowledge the abortion as the death of her child so that her grief becomes suppressed. There can be no real grieving, after all, if there is no one to grieve for. Interestingly, many of the 'pro-choice' agencies now advise women to grieve for the *potential* life which she has ended. These agencies are aware of and concerned about the harm done by suppressed grief in aborted women. (Their logic, however, is a little peculiar. I am not aware of any other case in which it is suggested that you can grieve for someone with whom you have never had a relationship. Nor did I ever hear of anyone having a relationship with a 'potential'.) The value of being allowed to grieve, even if it is only for a 'potential', is real but limited. It can only go so far. It cannot embrace all that has been lost or heal the breach between a mother and her child as long as the child is still not acknowledged as such.

Most aborted women do not allow themselves even this much release. They bury their wounds and give the outward appearance of being untouched by their experience. The alternative is to acknowledge grief, shock and loss – emotions which accompany death. Death occurs only where there has been life and if there has been life then a woman has had a living offspring who is now dead. This fact is the one above all others which cannot be acknowledged. Thus there can be no grief, no shock, no real loss. These will all be suppressed. They do not cease to be real, however, just because a woman denies their existence. She will simply experience their effects without admitting their source. As a result, many of the feelings she experiences will become 'disassociated' emotions.

I have seen these take the form of depression, phobia and compulsive behaviour whose root cause is simply not recognised. How *can* a woman recognise it unaided? Women who have abortions are not peculiar or inhuman. They are usually just frightened or pressured or miserable or all three. It is a nightmare for any normal woman to think that she has deliberately had her own offspring killed. She cannot think it, but all the same the horror will not disappear. I have met a woman haunted for twenty years by it. Bitter, angry, terrified, she had come for help, to talk about what the abortion had done to her and she was still unable to speak about the actual abortion.

In the months and years that followed the death of my own child, I travelled the same path as perhaps hundreds of thousands of other women, reliving the memories of pregnancy and abortion, seeing myself through the eyes of guilt and condemnation, wondering about the child who might have been born if I had allowed it. I could deal with my memories, however, because they were not nightmares for me. I was no longer afraid that I might have a dead child, or that I might have violated both my relationship with that child and my own being. I was not afraid these things were true. I knew that they *were* true, but I did not need to run from their implications. For me,

138

the implications had changed. Someone had given me back a sense of my own worth, had taken the punishment that I felt was due to me. Someone had taken the sting out of my memories and helped me to start putting my life back together, to believe that I was capable of living it as a finer person.

But who will help the ones who are trapped by memories they cannot face, the ones who live with suppressed grief and guilt, with the fear that they have destroyed more than a 'potential'? Someone must. The cycle of fear continues for many, many aborted women because so many people believe it is kind to repeat the rhetoric of the abortion mills. 'It was for the best.' 'It was the least bad of a set of bad choices.' 'It wasn't an actual baby yet.' 'There wasn't any other option.' And all the time there is the emptiness and the voice of accusation and the possibility of something too terrible to bear that haunts you because you can't turn and face it alone. And people are much too 'kind' to want to help you to face that kind of pain.

Chapter Ten

Healing

And so we come to healing – and the 'kindness' of other people. It has to be said that the source of such 'kindness' is usually an unwillingness to accept abortion as the horror story it really is. Faced with a suffering woman, much the most comfortable conclusion for anyone who wants to help her, is that her pain is unnecessary. Then it is just a matter of getting her to see that the abortion was really the right thing to do and that she hasn't really lost a baby, just a potential. Maybe she can be sad about the lost potential. And then she can get on with her life.

It doesn't usually work like that though. A woman may try her best to see it this way – really want to see it this way – but no matter how hard she tries, she will still be haunted by her nightmares, by her grief and doubt and guilt. The trouble is that our nice, helpful people are using their own terms of reference in order to help her, terms which just cannot explain or alleviate the reality which the woman herself is facing.

Now most nice people don't want to believe that the cause of her distress is actually the violent death of a tiny child and the violation of her motherhood. They do not want to believe it for two reasons. In the first place they wouldn't know how to begin helping a woman who is suffering because her baby has been deliberately killed. How many people would? So they prefer not to see it that way. In the second place, if they did see it that way, then they would have to accept that they lived in – and were part of – a society which daily enacts a grisly ritual of violation and death in hospitals and clinics throughout the land. That is not a nice reality to believe in. Nice people just won't have it, won't accept it.

It would be far better if abortion didn't happen in the first place. Once it has happened, however, the only way to help a woman who is in distress about it is to face the nightmare with her. Just doing that takes a certain amount of courage. It is a very ugly nightmare full of doors that lead to all kinds of horrible and heartbreaking possibilities. Let me give you some examples. If these aborted children are really just as human as you or I, did they have the same will to live? What degree of sensation and emotion do they experience? How much does it hurt them, how much does it terrify them to be killed in the womb? No one has the answers to these questions, so the very worst scenario you can imagine – full consciousness of pain and fear – remains possible. Recent research has suggested that the early neural development of the foetus is such that it feels not less, but more than the fully developed child. This has not been proved, but then neither has it been disproved – and there's the rub. It is the 'what if?' that no one can allay which makes the memory of an abortion so ghastly.

Very often the woman herself does not know what, in the memory of her abortion, is causing her most pain. It will not help her if the person she turns to for help does not have the courage or honesty to face the possibilities themselves. She has to face the worst of her own imaginings and you have to know what it is she is facing. (Given a little time and patience and an attitude that is completely accepting and non-judgemental, she will usually find the root of it herself, without any prompting from you.)

About two years ago I had lunch with a colleague and a friend of hers, whom I will call Peggy. I had never met her before. After lunch we returned to the office and my colleague began to ask about the effects of abortion on women. In response to her questioning I said that I had never met a woman who had not been badly hurt by an abortion. Peggy broke into the conversation at that point to say that she thought she must be the exception. She had had an abortion at fifteen and the experience had never troubled her since. I agreed that there had to be exceptions, it was just that I had not met any before meeting her. I asked her to tell me what had happened, and in a bright matter-of-fact voice she told her story.

She had become pregnant at fifteen. Her mother had been very ill at the time and had insisted that if Peggy had the baby it would kill her. So Peggy had an abortion. After the operation she had been using the bed pan when she began bleeding and passing heavy clots. When she looked to see what was happening to her, she found that the 'clots' were tiny pieces of baby: part of an arm, a hand, a foot – all miniature but perfect.

She paused there waiting, I think, for a reaction of disgust or distaste – something which would have confirmed this unpleasant 'medical experience'. Instead I said quietly, 'I'm terribly sorry. That must have been a dreadful shock for a fifteen-year-old.'

Peggy burst into tears and for some minutes she sobbed as if heartbroken. And out poured her hatred for her mother, her fear of relationships, her loneliness, her feeling of inadequacy. My colleague sat in silent amazement. Ever since she had known her, Peggy had had a problem with alcohol, with her relationships with men and a powerful and apparently irrational hatred of her mother. When she was calmer I suggested that Peggy have post-abortion counselling to try to get over the trauma which she had suffered and tried to ignore sixteen years before! She was clearly embarrassed by what had happened and told us that this was the first time she had ever wept about the abortion, the first time she had ever realised that she had such strong feelings about it. I don't know whether she went for counselling or not, but I do know that she took a first and most important step that afternoon. Peggy, the 'exception', had faced her own hidden nightmare.

Looking the horror squarely in the face is the first step. Sometimes, as in Peggy's case, it can take a long time for a woman to get that far. Sometimes she will be in agony because she has already faced the horror and she can get no further. I can give a more recent example of this, which might also serve to illustrate the remaining steps in post-abortion healing.

I had a phone call concerning a young woman living in a town near me. I contacted her and drove out the same night to see her. Meg was in her late twenties with two young children. She had had a difficult birth with both children. Her husband had just been made redundant when she became pregnant for a third time. It had been sheer bad luck, it seemed, because she was taking the contraceptive pill, had not missed taking it and had not been ill or taken any other medication which could have caused the pill to stop working. Her doctor arranged for her to have an abortion almost as a matter of course. And the abortion had devastated her. Her husband was distraught and the life of the whole family was being disrupted by her almost constant depression.

Meg was red-eyed when I arrived. She had been crying almost solidly for two days. Apparently this had become a regular feature of her life since the abortion six months before. As we talked, it became obvious that Meg wasn't running from any of the pain or the ugliness of the abortion. Instead she was methodically opening every door in that nightmare, envisaging every scenario and punishing herself with it. It was also obvious that she had reached a crisis point and there was no time to go step by step with her at a gentle pace. We had to cover the same ground in one evening that would normally take several weeks.

Just persuading her to trust me in that time might have been difficult, so I took a risk. I described some of the things I knew she might be experiencing but which she had not talked about. It worked. I think it convinced her that I really did understand what she was going through – and, perhaps, also that there wasn't any point in hiding her worst fears if I already knew them! She spoke of the baby 'crying out to her' as she went for the abortion. She 'knew' it must have been calling to her because she had been crying herself as she was admitted to the hospital. She spoke of how loveless and hard she must have been to go through with the abortion, how deceived she had been about what it would be like after the abortion was over. She spoke of the fact that she had not wanted the baby, had not loved the baby and then sobbed, 'But I did, I did love her. I just didn't know it.' (That hit home. I certainly remembered that realisation.) She described how unfit she felt she was to care for or even to touch her other children. She had spared herself nothing.

There was a real danger that the horror and self-hatred she was experiencing would overwhelm her and there was very little time in which to try to change her outlook. Still we went carefully, establishing what she really felt, what she really believed. In those three hours we established the extent of her own moral responsibility for what had happened (which was far less than she had assumed); the extent to which she herself was a victim (far greater than she had realised); and the fact that she regretted the abortion and would undo it if she could. We even managed to establish that the awfulness of abortion did not automatically make her an awful person. She volunteered the information that she was a Christian and she had recently been thinking about going back to church. That would make life a lot easier. (You have to work with a person's own, existing relationship with God, however limited you think it is. You can't try to give them yours.)

In the end, we were able to cover most of the ground which needed to be explored: saying sorry, believing that you are forgiven and accepted, accepting that there is no one left to condemn you since neither your child nor God condemns you; being allowed to love and mourn your dead child; believing that she is living and real in the next life and, finally, accepting and forgiving yourself. Meg was sure her baby was a girl, but giving her a name was too painful for her even to think about. All the same we had gone over far more than I had thought possible. And something happened as we talked, a shift in perspective — a door opening that might lead into hope instead of despair; I don't know how to describe it. But it happened. We were talking about her daughter as still being a member of her family and Meg said: 'That's beautiful — if it can really be like that.'

The battle was over. From that moment Meg would have something with which to counter the images of horror and death. I left at around eleven o'clock that night — by which time we were both exhausted.

The next day Meg was admitted to the psychiatric ward of the local hospital — but she was released less than a week later. Now she gets up in the morning and she doesn't spend her days in tears. She has not named the baby yet because she is finding the mourning painful. She still wants this baby. Naming her is part of accepting her death and Meg isn't ready to let her go yet. It will take time and I know that we will have to cover old ground, probably

145

many times. But the point will come, soon I hope, when she will accept her daughter's death and then want to cope on her own. I will be redundant, which is as it ought to be, although, just like the rest of us, Meg will have to go on dealing with painful reminders. But the worst of Meg's nightmare is over. It would have been better if it had never begun.

Except for one thing. The healing of something so fundamentally inhuman as abortion offers a practical lesson in real-life miracles. For those who believe in God, the impossible becomes possible. Our greatest crimes become the means by which we experience the greatest proofs of God's belief in and love for us. We can discover that death and loss are already cancelled out by that love. All things, all dreams, are possible through it. And the discovery of this truth, even through something as terrible as the destruction of an unborn child, is the discovery of a revelation which can change the way we see all death, all loss and even the way in which we see ourselves. And that is a discovery well worth making.

Appendix
Post-Abortion Trauma and its Causes

This brief overview of post-abortion trauma and its causes may help to give a clearer picture of the experience I describe in chapter 5. More importantly, it will establish that experience in its place as a single example of a much wider and largely unrecognised phenomenon. Without such an overview this book would be just 'one woman's story' and it would say nothing about what lies behind the distress of thousands of other women. It would explain too little about the 'mechanics' of post-abortion trauma or the principles of post-abortion healing. And there would be no compelling reason to suppose that anyone else might have had the same kind of experience.

As a matter of fact, for a long time after the abortion it seemed to me that mine *was* a unique experience that no one else could understand, let alone share. Even in this misapprehension I was simply following the pattern of many aborted women. Over 100,000 abortions take place in Britain each year and yet one experience which many aborted women have in common is that of isolation. Part of the reason for this has to do with the mental walls which certainly I, and many others I have spoken to, built as a defence against what we had done. And part of the reason has to do with the nature of suffering.

There is something deeply private about our own pain. We experience suffering, in fact, as something so personal that we are liable to be surprised when we discover that other people have suffered the same sort of unhappiness. And yet we do need to know that we are not alone in our pain, however private it may be. We need to know that there are others we can talk to who understand exactly what we are going through. There are all sorts of support groups and self-help groups which exist simply because of this need. One of the most important messages which they try to put across is the one which says, 'You are not alone in your pain.'

These groups depend a great deal on good publicity to reach those they want to help. I don't just mean publicity about the organisations themselves, but about the very conditions which have brought them into being: mental handicap, child abuse, alcoholism in the family, miscarriage, physical handicap and so on. Publicity creates social awareness of a problem, of the fact that help is available and most of all of the fact that there are many others who are experiencing the same trauma.

Publicity about post-abortion trauma is almost non-existent and so, therefore, is any social awareness of the problem. Thus many aborted women who feel alone in the aftermath of abortion will continue to do so, sometimes for years. It simply does not seem possible that anyone else might have experienced the same things – might have had the same sorts of problems and emotions during pregnancy, the same patterns of guilt and depression after abortion. The very fact of post-abortion trauma is ignored or denied in our society, so there can be no discussion of its effects or of what is contained in the nature of deliberate abortion which causes such distress.

Abortion, in turn, is not generally perceived as being violent and traumatic. But then it is not portrayed that way, either by the media or the medical profession. Abortion may be seen as an emotional subject, but it is still a reasonably 'polite' one. The problems it raises are debated as if they were only religious, philosophical or ethical. Brutality, force and destruction are not acknowledged as being any part of the reality of abortion and neither is the grief or despair of many women who choose it. As a result we experience post-abortion trauma like a prison sentence spent in solitary confinement. This is not only my own experience, but that of many counsellors, doctors, researchers and writers working with, or studying, the after-effects of abortion.

Without suggesting any conscious conspiracy to suppress the truth, it has to be said that our comfortable, polite image of abortion (and, of course, of those who perform or facilitate abortions) would be seriously undermined if the media or the medical profession were to acknowledge the massive emotional and psychological damage which has, in fact, been done to thousands of women by that 'safe' legal procedure.

It took me a long time, six years in fact, before I really began to compare my own experience of abortion with that of other women, and then it was almost by accident — mostly through meeting and talking to other aborted women. Gradually I began to be aware and then surprised that I had not met anyone who had had an abortion who was not still deeply affected by it. I realised that no matter what our positions or opinions on abortion as an issue, we had all shared something in common, something that looked very like grief. And one thing became clear from my conversations with other aborted women, with post-abortion counsellors and from the increasing mass of literature on the subject. Abortion is never just 'over and done with'. It goes on affecting all sorts of areas of your life: your self-image, your belief in yourself, your ability to form lasting relationships, your attitude to children, your attitude to death. It can interfere with any and all of these – and more.

Many women have spoken of the feeling of emptiness after an abortion (a feeling which I remember well). This may give way to an increasing sense of loss, depression and then to fear and anger. Or it may become all of these. It may be a reaction which remains buried in the subconscious or one which becomes a constant daily struggle with despair. Post-abortion trauma typically manifests itself in a number of ways and its severity varies according to the circumstances, emotional strength, well-being or sensitivity of the individual woman. This book is not a scientific textbook and this is not the place to quote lists of statistics and medical studies. The following post-abortion distress patterns have been documented by various studies and reflect the experiences of numerous writers – including my own and that of other aborted women I have met.

1. *Emotional paralysis* – inability to express feelings, sometimes even to communicate at all. This is frequently the result of the suppression or denial of the feelings of grief, loss and guilt which are generally experienced by women after an abortion.

2. *Psychosomatic illness* can also be the result of suppressed feelings of remorse after an abortion. Self-inflicted illness among aborted women has been found to include abdominal pain, dysmenorrhea, vomiting, ulcers and anorexia.

3. *Depression*, sadness or a sense of loss are common soon after an abortion. Mostly these feelings fade after a while, but occasionally they continue and worsen. More often they return in later years as black moods, feelings of isolation, sometimes frequent crying and sometimes

complete withdrawal and despair. The depression can be so severe that an affected woman will entertain frequent thoughts of suicide. The following is an extract of a reply printed on the advice page of a national British newspaper:

> An anonymous letter from a distraught young girl is making me tear my hair with anxiety about her. The only clue I have is the postmark ... She begged me to help her through her depression, explaining that she was persuaded against her will to have an abortion. Both she and her boy friend wanted the baby. But the pressures put on her by her family were more than she could withstand. Now, she says, she can't stop crying and doesn't want to live any more. I long to be able to write to this unhappy girl, to try to reassure her and give her hope for the future.[5]

4. *Guilt and remorse*. Guilt and remorse are among the most common of reported reactions to abortion. Guilt is the first stage of feeling badly about what you have done, but it doesn't necessarily mean that you cannot live with yourself. Remorse is agonising. It is self-recrimination, the unforgiving 'if only...' on the grand scale. The pro-abortion lobby frequently claims that guilt about abortion is a Western phenomenon, a social hang-up left over from centuries of exposure of puritanical Christianity. If abortion were available on demand, they argue, and if society didn't condemn abortion, then aborted women would not suffer from guilt and remorse. But guilt is cross-cultural, appearing as powerfully and as frequently in Japan, for instance (which has had abortion on demand for decades and which is not a Christian culture), as it does in the West.

5. *Anxiety or fear* is almost as common as guilt. It may be accompanied by insomnia and/or nightmares about the abortion or the aborted child. Occasionally it is

acute, producing feelings of terror and panic – commonly a fear of death – and even, in some cases, psychotic or schizophrenic reactions.

6. *Low self-esteem* is often expressed through destructive behaviour which may include the use of drugs, increased use of alcohol and promiscuity. Self-punishment is often associated with this type of behaviour:

> Whether it is the result of having compromised their own values or having further weakened their poor self-images, many aborted women develop patterns of self-destructive behaviour in order to punish themselves for their 'unworthiness'. Such self-destructive behaviour, called symbolic suicide, may include abuse of alcohol and drugs. Some may become obsessed with food and try to 'eat their way into oblivion' or 'to fill' the great emptiness they feel inside themselves. Still others may develop anorexia nervosa in a subconscious attempt to starve or 'fast' themselves to death.[4]

The notion and even expectation of punishment is closely bound up with the self-image of the aborted woman. She may perceive herself as a criminal, as a failure, an inadequate mother and an inadequate human being deserving of punishment and unworthy of love, affection or approval.

> Those who mention God in speaking of their guilt express two points of view. Some believe that they are forgiven by God but cannot forgive themselves. Others believe that God is punishing them through infertility, miscarriages, or through other emotional conflicts in their lives.[5]

7. *Anger*; usually expressed to the partner or others perceived as 'accomplices' in the abortion. Blaming the partner, parent or anyone else involved in arranging or performing the abortion is another common pattern

among aborted women. In fact very few relationships survive the abortion of a couple's child, the woman often feeling betrayed and unsupported by her partner.

8. Sexual dysfunction. While promiscuity is a part of the self-destructive behaviour of some women after abortion, sexual inhibition in women is an alternative pattern. This symptom can manifest itself years after an abortion in cases where the initial feelings of guilt and grief which follow abortion have been deeply suppressed.

> This finding prompted discussant Vincent Rue to equate Post-Abortion Distress Syndrome with Post Traumatic Distress Syndrome, which was identified in veterans of the Vietnam War. The latter syndrome results from the initial suppresssion and denial of physical and psychological trauma on the battlefield, which reasserts itself in psychological disorders at a later time.[6]

For some women post-abortion trauma sets in shortly after the abortion itself, while for others the symptoms may only occur in later life. In fact it is more usual for there to be a delay between abortion and the onset of post-abortion distress. It can be triggered by the anniversary of the abortion, or the expected date of birth of the dead child; by the birth of a subsequent baby or the birth of a friend's or relative's baby and sometimes by the onset of the menopause. While I believe that it affects all aborted women to a greater or lesser degree, for some it may not cause serious disruption or even interfere with day-to-day living. The effects of an abortion, however, are cumulative and a subsequent trauma of any kind, or changes in a woman's circumstances or emotional state, can trigger severe abortion-related depression years after the event. This is largely because so many women suppress their negative feelings about abortion. But the longer they do so, the worse seems to be the distress when it finally surfaces.

A considerable body of literature exists which addresses the problem of post-abortion psychological sequelae. The duration of post-abortion distress among some women is substantial. A group of Canadian researchers examined one hundred and twenty two women who had experienced induced abortion.[7]

The long lapse of time reported among the above sample of women experiencing post-abortion sequelae has been noted on other studies. Cases include a woman of forty-five whose distress about an abortion twenty years in her past was exacerbated by her reaching the end of her childbearing years.[8]

There are many people who claim that while it may have a negative effect in the short term, in the long term abortion does not create any intrinsic problems of its own – beyond the physical complications which some women may suffer. They would say that any persistent or extreme psychological trauma is caused by the woman's state of mind, her attitude, rather than what is, after all, not the death of a child but only 'the loss of a potential life'. Women who suffer suicidal depression after an abortion do so, by this way of thinking, because they were not properly counselled before the operation and/or because of religious, anti-abortion propaganda which associates abortion with sin and guilt.

This is just wishful thinking. Abortion is violence and death and loss, and in one way or another these things are bound to have more than a theoretical effect. It is the women, the other victims of abortion, who must live with their effects, while society continues to pretend that they do not exist.

One of the saddest things about post-abortion trauma is that many women have simply swallowed the prevailing line, believing that if society says abortion is OK then it really can't be all that bad. If abortion killed babies then doctors wouldn't do it – right? Wrong. It is just that a lot of doctors don't see the developing foetus as a human person, not in the same way that a newborn infant is a person. Nobody warns a woman who 'chooses' abortion that if it is a 'personal decision' when you think a foetus becomes a baby, then that decision might change in the future. You might accept the doctor's view when you have an abortion and then find that you don't really believe it later on when it is too late. The fact that you may have been misled, however, doesn't lessen post-abortion trauma one bit.

There is an anger growing among women who have been deceived by pro-abortion rhetoric, who have lost their children, who feel that they have lost part of themselves. It is an anger which needs to be heard, from the halls of the Houses of Parliament to the doors of the abortion clinics. It is expressed for me in the story of a friend of mine who had suffered an early miscarriage. When she could not stop crying afterwards a nurse came and told her not to be so stupid because 'it was only a blob of cells'. My friend replied furiously, 'It may be a blob to you, but it was *my* baby.'

We do need to cut through the rhetoric and understand the human reality of what is happening to women, as well as the violence done to their children, through abortion. That will not happen, however, at least not on a wide scale, until enough women have recovered from abortion and can tell the world what is really happening.

There are some professional psychologists and doctors (at the other extreme from those who deny the existence of post-abortion trauma), who claim that the problems which abortion creates for a woman can never be resolved. They are wrong. It is true that they base their conclusions on the evidence of growing numbers of women whom they have seen or even treated as patients. But abortion as a problem on a massive scale has only been with us for a very short time, less than half a century. Post-abortion trauma is only only beginning to be recognised as a real and deeply destructive syndrome. It is a little strange to suppose that of all the afflicted who have ever lived, aborted women alone ought to be able to find the way to their own healing, and that if they do not it means that there is no such healing to be found. It is also a little premature to say that because no methodology of post-abortion healing has yet been established, therefore none exists to be discovered. I chose to write this book, not out of the hope that women can be healed from abortion, but out of the knowledge that they can.

There was no one I could or would have talked to about my feelings after the abortion. I blanked out the memory, built walls around my emotions and tried to ignore them. Nevertheless these discarded parts of me continued to affect everything I did, my whole outlook on life and all my relationships. But I doubt if anyone had the slightest idea there was anything at all wrong with me. I might have gone on like that for years, I suppose, if I had not been very fortunate. I have no rational explanation for what happened, and those who do not accept the existence of anything we might call supernatural will certainly believe that the whole event was the product of my own mind. You must draw your own conclusion.

Notes

1. Richardson and Dixon, 'Effects of legal termination on subsequent pregnancy', *British Medical Journal*, 1976, 1, 1303–1304.
2. 'Femail', *Daily Mail*, 7th December, 1989.
3. *Daily Mirror*, 19th August, 1986.
4. David C Reardon, *Aborted Women, Silent No More* (Illinois: Crossway Books, 1987), p 128.
5. *Ibid.*
6. Post-Abortion Distress Syndrome Analysed', *National Right to Life News*, June 1986.
7. Ian Kent *et al*, 'Emotional Sequelae of Therapeutic Abortions; A Comparative Study', *North Carolina Medical Journal*.
8. Mary Parthun, msw, 'Abortion's Aftermath; The Psychological Effects of Induced Abortion', Human Life Research Institute Reports, no 2.